Let Sleeping Dogs Lie

Let Sleeping Dogs Lie

Mirjam Pressler

TRANSLATED BY Erik J. Macki

Front Street
Asheville, North Carolina

Printed in China
Designed by Helen Robinson
First U.S. edition, 2007

The translation of this work was supported by a grant from the Goethe-Institut that is funded by the Ministry of Foreign Affairs, Germany.

Library of Congress Cataloging-in-Publication Data
Pressler, Mirjam.
[Die zeit der schlafenden Hunde. English]
Let sleeping dogs lie / by Mirjam Pressler ;
translated by Erik J. Macki.
p. cm.
ISBN 978-1-932425-84-0
(hardcover : alk. paper)
I. Macki, Erik J. II. Title.
PT2676.R394Z4513 2006
833'.914—dc22 2006101752

Front Street
An Imprint of Boyds Mills Press, Inc.
815 Church Street
Honesdale, Pennsylvania 18431

For Ursula. And Frank.

Prologue

In the morning, when you can see the brightness even though your eyelids are still closed, when you stretch still warm under the covers, when you sleepily tense up your muscles and relax them again, it's easy to be happy.

Johanna fumbles next to her, eyes still closed, but her fingers feel only fabric, the smooth pillowcase yielding under her touch, the sheet, a bit rougher, rumpled, and untucked at the corner, the comforter pulled all the way up to the pillow over the spot where Daniel had lain, as though there were something to hide, a memory that warmed her face. Daniel isn't here anymore, he snuck out of the house after midnight, after her parents had already gone to sleep. She's alone even though she can still smell skin and sweat and happiness, she can still feel his hands, his breath in her hair.

He had come over late in the afternoon. They did their English homework, read articles out loud to each other from the *New York Times* and the *Observer*, analyzed the texts, and discussed a presentation for class on the economic situation in the countries of South America. After dinner they worked some more, then all at once they landed in bed, just as naturally as before, as though time had turned back, as though the past few months had not existed, as though it were spring again and they still had summer to look forward to. Nothing stood between them, no shadow, no guilt—which Daniel doesn't know anything about anyway and never will—like when he used to come over and laugh, when she could still just laugh with him.

She opens her eyes, slowly wafting out of sleep to alight again in her room, which she loves. *My room is my castle,* she thinks as her gaze wanders over the far wall with bookcases up to the window, framing a blue sky. *Today's going to be a beautiful day.*

I've got to put it behind me, she reasons, *I've got to become that happy-go-lucky girl I used to be before April—having fun, going out and doing things, being easygoing, doing normal stuff. It can't be that hard, those things used to be part of me, you don't just lose it all. I've got to rediscover joy again, it's just been pushed aside by what some old woman said. I have to wipe her words off me the way you wipe dust off your pants when you trip and get up again. I'm not responsible for what happened such a long time before I was born—it's been fifty-seven years, half an eternity, it's been so long. I don't want to forget you, Mrs. Levin, certainly not. I'll go to Israel, my plans haven't changed, but you've got to accept that I'm a separate person, an autonomous person, not just the granddaughter of Erhard Riemenschneider.*

She gets too hot under the covers, she stands up, walks naked over to the window, opens it, feels the cool air on her skin, and breathes in and out deeply. Now in the light of early morning, the city's buildings still have oddly soft shapes, as though you were looking at them through a filter, nothing stark, everything in matching tones, almost melting into one another. This is a view she knows well. She has stood at this spot at least two or three times a day for years, ever since she moved into what used to be her father's workroom, she has stood here looking out over the houses on the other side of the street, she knows every rooftop, every tree, both of the high-rises over by the train station, the river that peeks through here and there amid the snarl of houses.

She knows the blocks farther on, around the freight station, she knows the roofs of the old medieval part of town, which you can make out clearly even from here.

The four pointy gable windows facing the open-air market on Marktplatz are a part of Riemenschneider's Fine Apparel, Coats & Leather, the store her family has run since the early 1800s. The building is registered as a national historic landmark, so when they'd renovated it, its façade of rough-hewn sandstone and magnificent window ledges couldn't be changed. Behind the gable windows, the garret rooms on the third floor house the storage area. She had worked there herself on vacations and found the rooms quite pretty. When she was little, her father had lived up in those rooms for a few years with her grandfather until the family moved into the new house on Fischmarkt.

"You're getting the room with the nicest view," her father had said five years ago as he was moving his desk out of the attic into the old playroom downstairs. Florian was getting her old room on the second floor. "The rest of us get to see only the neighbors' houses, but you'll have the whole town beneath you when you look out the window, the whole town and even the store."

The store, she thinks. *Everything in our lives revolves around the store.* She's known for a while that this isn't the life she wants. Even before her trip to Israel, even if she hadn't decided on anything specific, she knew there were so many things she could do instead. Daniel wants to major in physics, Kerstin wants to be a doctor, Melanie a librarian, and all she knows is that she doesn't want to go into the family business, even though her parents take it so much for granted that they don't even question it. Obviously, she can go to school and major in something, they say. Business management wouldn't be a bad option if she doesn't want to go to the fashion design school, even law school is a possibility. "As if!" Johanna protests. "You guys are in for a shock."

She can just make out the clatter of dishes from the kitchen downstairs, it's just a hint of noise, nothing more, but it tells her that she'd better hurry. She takes a shower, pulls on the blue T-shirt she knows Daniel particularly likes, pairing it with her faded jeans. She hesitates just a moment in front of the bed, wondering if she should change the sheets so Mrs. Maurer, the cleaning lady, won't find any damning evidence, but then she thinks how nice it'll be to still feel some of last night's passion when she goes to sleep tonight. With a few jerks she pulls the sheet smooth, fluffs the pillow, and arranges the comforter neatly on top. *Check this out, Mrs. Maurer, my bed is already made, and what's hidden under the covers belongs to the night and isn't any of your business.*

She stoops, picks up the underwear and socks from her yellow rug she loves so much because its color and pattern remind her of a mosaic in progress, bathed in Mediterranean light, whose scattered stones don't yet know the role they will play in the finished picture that so far exists only in the mind of the unknown artist. She picked the rug out three years ago after she had come back from a trip to Pompeii, four days of just her and her mother, a gift for her fifteenth birthday.

As she walks past the bathroom on the second floor, she hears the water of the shower rushing. It's her father, usually the last one ready in the morning.

Mom has set the table already. They always have breakfast right in the kitchen, no one has time before school and work to be running back and forth between the kitchen and the dining room. As usual, Florian is sitting there half-asleep and grumpy, watching how honey drips from the spoon onto his bread. Mom is standing at the sideboard writing a note to Mrs. Maurer.

"Morning," says Johanna, pouring herself a cup of coffee and sitting down at the table.

"Good morning," says her mother. "You two were up studying for quite a while last night, I didn't even hear Daniel leave."

Johanna doesn't respond. Her mother made the remark casually, without any hidden accusation, without expecting an answer. Johanna sips her coffee, feels it running down her throat and spreading through her, a warm, pleasant feeling as though everything, everything were OK again.

The telephone in the hallway rings. When her father comes down the stairs, she can see him through the open kitchen door taking a couple of steps toward the chest and lifting the receiver. "Hello?" he says skeptically, almost annoyed, because who in the world would be calling so early, and then he doesn't say anything for a long time.

Johanna sees his face change, his lips, much too full for a man, move apart from each other, the upper lip moving up, the lower lip moving down, as if he were baring his teeth, and this expression stays on his face the whole time he's listening. A strange, tense silence unfolds, as if time were fixed. Even Mom stops writing to turn her shoulders and stare at Dad. Johanna senses that something dangerous, crippling is forcing its way out of the receiver into the house, something that is changing even her father's voice, stretching out his words like an old cassette tape being played back too slowly, when he says, "Yes, that's right. Please do that, the number is on top of the list. I'll be there within the hour."

She watches him slowly hang up, uncertain, cautious, his fingers tentative, pointed as though he were going to flick a bug back onto the grass in the yard, and then he takes a step forward, with outstretched arms, standing in the doorway, leaning on the frame as though he couldn't hold himself up anymore, and still in that strange voice without looking at anyone says, "That was Mrs. Tschernowski. He's dead. He hanged himself. In the garret. She just found him."

Johanna looks from her father to her mother, to her brother. No one says anything. The silence is unbearable, and everything around her seems to crumble to pieces, the faces turn to grimaces, objects melt together. She stares at the coffee cup, and her hands, which had just been enjoying the warmth from the porcelain, now suddenly stiffen as though she were holding a lump of ice. She thinks, *Now it's happened, now I can't act like nothing's wrong anymore.*

White Roses

Everyone is standing there around the open grave. The sky is gray, still, even if a couple of blue patches are showing through the clouds. It rained last night, and this morning when she opened the window she saw the thin threads of rain and thought, *How fitting, he's managed even this. The perfect weather for his funeral.*

She's wearing the black dress her mother brought home from the store for her yesterday, although she would have preferred to wear her normal clothes—jeans, a T-shirt, if necessary the black jacket she's now wearing over the dress—but her mother didn't think it was appropriate. Even Florian had to put on a black suit. He fought against the tie, and Mom gave in when Dad finally said, "Just let him be, he's only twelve, after all."

So now everyone's standing here around the open grave, most of them in black or dark blue or gray, and Johanna thinks, *Apparently, funerals still require special attire, they all look like they're wearing uniforms.* And their faces, which are pale, as though they'd lost their tans overnight, are each as expressionless as the next.

Standing behind the relatives, neighbors, bank managers, members of the chamber of commerce, behind the doctors, both of the pharmacists who they alternate getting their refills from, behind all the businesspeople who "won't deny their old competitor one last honor," as her mother put it, are most of the forty-three employees of Riemenschneider's. The store is closed today, the older employees who had still worked under her grandfather were invited to the banquet in honor of their deceased boss, and, at her mother's request, the trainees were, too. "It ties them to the store," she said, and Johanna thought, *People do the right thing when it's in their own best interest.*

A wind springs up, the ribbons on the wreaths that will soon be lying on the mound of earth flutter for a moment before they sink back onto the sprigs of fir. A sickeningly sweet smell hangs over the cemetery. Johanna doesn't know whether it's coming from the wreaths or flower arrangements, or from perfume or aftershave. It reminds her how her grandfather used to smell whenever the disease wasn't tangling up his mind, suddenly turning him into a hobo, disheveled, rarely shaven, and, as her mother would endlessly complain, "smelling unpleasantly of sweat and old man."

"Oh, why'd he do it," whispers Aunt Irene, his sister, much too loudly, opening her black handbag and rustling a fresh tissue out of the package.

"Will you be quiet," hisses Uncle Peter, her husband. "You don't have to be broadcasting that in public. You heard what Robert said, nobody needs to know about it."

And Aunt Amalia says, "Hey, Reverend, *pssst*, let's get things going," then leans heavily on Uncle Erwin's arm.

I don't know if he would have wanted the minister, thinks Johanna. *He never went to church, at most once a year at Christmas or for weddings and funerals.* She hears the voice of her mother ringing in her ears, "Sometimes it's the right thing to do, should we just dump some dirt on him?" *That's what people used to do with suicides*, Johanna had thought, and her father had said, "Ultimately, he is a highly regarded man." *Was,* she had thought. *Was, you've got to get used to your father being dead.*

"… a highly regarded man," the minister is also saying just now, speaking about his "childhood of privation in impoverished circumstances," an "assiduous and hardworking man. With the labor of his own hands he worked his way up, achieving prosperity and respect." And she thinks, *What hypocrisy! Should I say the names Heimann and Rosenblatt out loud now? What would happen if I did, if I said, Hey, wait a minute there, Mr. Minister, you've overlooked something important, there's still a dark stain on the life of my grandfather, it wasn't as easy as all that, the story of his life doesn't just make a beeline from deprived childhood to wealthy businessman. It wasn't just the labor of his own hands, Mr. Minister, even if I don't know exactly what it was, actually, I don't even want to know, I don't want to know if Mrs. Levin was telling the truth. But there are a lot of old people here, and they've got to remember what really happened, if they haven't chosen to forget.* And she remembers what Daniel said once, "You've got to talk to him, you can't just go on pretending forever that nothing's wrong." She left him standing there and thought, *What business is it of mine? I'm going to be out of here in less than a year.*

As the minister continues to speak, her gaze passes over the mourners who are so numerous, so befitting the funeral of a highly regarded, wealthy citizen of the city. The image starts blurring before her eyes, the shapes lose their contours, dissolve, disappear into the gray horizon as the cemetery becomes his garden.

He was on his knees between the flower beds the last time she saw him, about three weeks ago. She can't remember what day it was anymore, maybe Wednesday, because she gets home a bit earlier on Wednesdays. “Can you go look in on Grandpa?” her mother had said. “Hasn’t checked in in a couple of days. You can take my car.” The offer was enticing to someone with a brand new driver’s license, just three months old, so she drove over.

She found him out in the garden, kneeling on the raked path between the beds and groaning, “My old bones aren’t cooperating anymore,” and she asked, “Why aren’t you having Mrs. Tschernowski do this, isn’t she here?”

He shook his head. “No, not at all this week. She went to Cologne to visit her daughter, who just had a baby, and the weeds keep growing and growing …” His voice faded into an unintelligible mumble, as it often did, and she didn’t know what to do.

She didn’t feel like helping him do this pointless chore. There was no reason an old, stiff-jointed man should be crawling around on the ground. The weeds could wait for Mrs. Tschernowski, or he could have just called and her father would have sent someone over.

“Shall I make us some coffee?” she asked, but he didn’t answer. He had apparently forgotten again she was there.

She sat down on the bench under the apple tree, rested her arms on the table where he would often sit when the weather was nice, and waited for him to remember her again. It was a pleasant day, not as hot as it had been in weeks previous. The apples were hanging small and green on the branches, covered in a whitish sheen, sort of like little slipcovers. She imagined how that sour light green would feel in her mouth, and it made her lips pucker.

She watched him grabbing between the flowers in agitated motions, ripping out the plants, both those that were weeds and those that were not weeds but prevented the flowers from growing, robbing them of their light, air, and food. She contemplated him, his bent back and angular shoulder blades moving under his light-colored shirt, his shoulders sunken forward, his mildly sunburned neck that turned white under his collar, his tan arms, his hands dotted with age spots and landscaped with meandering veins, dark and thick, so that you could almost see the slow-moving blood inside. As she watched him, pity swelled in her and pressed tears out of her eyes, but when he noticed her, the tears were dispelled by an abrupt, rising anger.

The way he pulled out the plants, without consideration for the tiny blue or white blossoms, without a sense for their tenderness, their innocence, their modesty, nurturing only the showy dahlias with their intense colors, the smug delphiniums, and the monkshood with its understated beauty, the way he gave no consideration to the tender roots, the white shoots that would end up withering helplessly in the air.

"Your grandma always wanted a garden," he said, suddenly remembering that Johanna was there. He raised his head, his white stubble shining in the light, reminding her of a cut field of wheat with tips already bleached by the sun. He wiped the sweat off his brow with his dirty fingers, leaving behind streaks of dirt, ugly streaks of dirt below his shiny, freckled bald head that she had loved so much when she was little. All at once her fingers stung, the memory of his smooth skin and of his skull that you could feel underneath turned her palms into fire, into an ache that she had lost the grandfather she once knew.

"Your grandma always wanted a garden," he said again, "but she passed away before we could afford one."

Then he grabbed into the weeds again, ripping out thick stalks, thin stalks, many of them so fragile they bent just from the touch of his gnarled fingers. Under his faint tan, his skin was a yellowish gray, like delicate tissue paper stretched tight over his skull. His ears were large, much larger than she remembered, and when he lifted his face up and looked at her, his eyes reflected the color of the sky. They were getting bluer and bluer as he got older. The patterns in his irises had faded, had lost any shading, the color wasn't broken by the shadow of his eyelashes anymore, he didn't have any eyelashes anymore. Naked eyes in a naked face. Even his bushy eyebrows had grown thin.

Earlier, much earlier, he had been blond. She knew the pictures of him standing there, blond and upright. Of course she knew them, she had looked through them often enough and thought what a handsome man he was. More handsome than her father, who, even as a child—the pictures prove it—had looked stockier. He had inherited his build and face from his mother, especially her mouth.

"Your grandmother always was a country girl," her grandfather said. "She would never have moved into town," and he wiped more sweat off his brow, the streaks of dirt suddenly looking like birthmarks. *Like marks of Cain*, she thought, regretting that she had come at all. The closeness they used to share had disappeared, even the dislike had disappeared. Any reproach was pointless before this old, naked face whose earlier beauty, hardness, and unexpected tenderness were no longer anywhere to be seen.

"He's gotten worse over the past few months," her father had said a couple of weeks ago. "He's getting noticeably worse. He doesn't understand things at all anymore, he should move into a good nursing home. He's got plenty of money, but he's as stubborn as a mule, always has been, so there's no talking to him about it."

"That's how it is sometimes with old people," her mother replied. "You'll get old eventually, too. It's natural to get old."

"If the right time to die doesn't come first," her father had said with a stiff expression, his lips hardly moving.

She had doubted for a moment whether he had really said those words, then she saw his face, saw how her mother's eyes narrowed, and she had stood up and walked out, leaving her parents alone in the living room, which had been fixed up last spring with newly reupholstered furniture, the slightly shiny material striped green and white, matching the new lime green rugs. The room looked fresh, almost cheery, very different from before when the furniture was still covered in brown and beige.

Music was coming out of Florian's room, techno. Music she could not stand, and it was too loud as well, otherwise she might have gone in, sat with him, and asked how his paper for English class had turned out. Maybe it was just as well that she hadn't. She was afraid of what he might have said, because she wouldn't have known how to respond in anything other than clichés, *There's always next time, you've got to put in a little effort,* trivialities. That's why she'd walked past his door, up the stairs, into her room.

"Your grandmother was a good woman," her grandfather said. "But that's how it is, the good die much too young. It's the ones God loves that he takes early, that's the way it's always been."

She bit her tongue, suddenly tasting blood in her mouth, it hurt so much not to speak the words that wanted to burst out of her. *It wasn't God who had taken her, she killed herself, that much at least I do know, even if I have no idea why, but she killed herself, she threw herself in front of the train, have you forgotten that? Is that your solution for everything—forgetting? Don't you have any other ideas at all?*

She just swallowed the words instead of speaking them, and when he tried in vain to get back on his feet, she didn't stand up to help him. She stayed seated and watched him scoot up to the bench on his knees, a degrading posture for his granddaughter to see, a shameful posture, like an old, lame dog.

Her mother gives her a nudge. "Johanna, please, people are looking." She lifts her head and sees that the wind has driven the clouds away, suddenly the sun is shining in her eyes, and the people standing around the grave all at once look too warmly dressed, black against the blooming flowers on the other graves, black against the wreaths, black against the blue sky.

She watches her father grab a shovel and tip soil into the grave three times, then pass the shovel to her mother. She feels the flowers in her hands burning, white roses—*why white roses, those are the flowers least suited to him, no white roses*—and now as she walks toward the open hole herself, for a moment behind the mound of soil she thinks she can make out the gold letters on a headstone, an inscription she already knows, which will be visible again only later after this new grave has been filled in—Johanna Katharina Riemenschneider, née Keller, 1915–1960—and the photograph materializes before her, the woman with her dark hair parted in the middle and pulled back tightly, the wide cheekbones, the blouse buttoned all the way up to the stand-up collar.

The woman in the picture is holding her baby up to the camera proudly, her son who was born late, who she waited so long for, her smile on strikingly full lips. *Too full to really be pretty*, Johanna thinks. She runs the tip of her tongue over her lips, the ones this woman left to her through her father, through the baby in the picture, and then she drops the roses into the hole, onto the dark casket with its gold fittings, thinking, *Why didn't you have him cremated and spread his ashes so that the wind could carry them to Israel and then Mrs. Levin will know that she can finally stop hating?*

The soil falls onto the white roses, and she can see the streaks of dirt on his forehead again, the mark of Cain she saw so recently. She's sweating and freezing at the same time. Her mother pushes her to the side and leads Florian to the grave. He has white roses in his hands as well.

"Good-bye, Grandpa," he says in his little boy's voice, still high yet not quite hiding a different tone, as if someone is lightly, just lightly touching the string on a bass, and the tone is resonating, not in any really audible way, but just enough to feel vibrations on the skin, not on the eardrum.

Friedrich Stamm, Uncle Friedrich, his friend, his only friend from youth, is escorted to the grave by his daughter. He can't really walk that well anymore since his heart attack last year. Johanna notices how old he looks—very, very old and frail, older than her grandfather had looked three weeks ago. Uncle Friedrich stumbles with nothing in his way, his legs bow inward, Johanna sees her father take a step forward and hold out his arms as if to protect the old man from falling into the grave. But his daughter holds him tight, with one hand she grabs for his, which is hanging over her shoulder, and with the other grips him tight around the waist so that it looks almost as if she's carrying him off. Uncle Friedrich is crying, he's the only one who's crying, as though he were the only person who loved him.

Then they're all standing there—Dad, Mom, her, Florian, Grandpa's sisters, Amalia and Irene—the relatives she hasn't wanted to belong to anymore ever since her trip to Israel, but here she is in full public view belonging to them, being his granddaughter, and the mourners are coming and taking her hand, saying, "I'm so sorry for your loss," and each of them, the relatives, says thank you before taking the hand of the next person. Sometimes Mom says, "We'll see you afterward at the Golden Goose," then the other person nods and says, "Yes, of course."

I don't want to be doing this, Johanna thinks, trying not to feel anything, but she nonetheless feels their hands, hard, soft, warm, cold, dry, clammy, and ideally she'd like to wipe her fingers off on her dress, like a little girl, to cleanse herself of all this invasive touching she so dislikes. But she doesn't pull her hand away, she continues to say, "Thank you," "Thank you," until her right hand turns into a foreign object that she can set into the hands that they hold out to her, while her left hand hangs down limply. She moves as if wound up, like a doll. Only when faced with the hand of Mrs. Neuberger, the wife of the pharmacist at the market, does she have to fight back tears for a moment because all at once she sees Mrs. Levin before her.

No one's crying. Her father wouldn't be anyway, but even her mother isn't, and she's normally quite liberal with her tears, and not even Florian, who's been crying so much the past few days. Now his face looks withdrawn, as though none of this has anything to do with him. *Maybe people don't cry in public for suicides*, Johanna thinks, amazed at how easy it is to think the word *suicide,* it's a word like any other: *suicide.*

Her father hadn't cried at all. "He must have had a lucid moment," he said after Mrs. Tschernowski called to say she had found him in the garret. "He was already very cold," he said with a stiff, dry expression. The only tears in the room were running down her mother's cheeks as she said, "How sad he must have felt, how alone."

They sat down to breakfast as though nothing were wrong,

but something was wrong, not one of the four of them ate anything, not even Florian, who hadn't quite understood everything that morning. Only later in the afternoon when he was sitting at the dining-room table doing his homework had he suddenly started to sob.

"I'm going to drive right over," Dad said. "I'll take care of everything." And when Mom asked, "Should I come with you?" he said, "No, you go to the store, after all, someone's got to break it to the staff—and think about what the obituary in the paper should say, and maybe you could start working on the list of people we absolutely have to send a personal funeral card to. Johanna, can you stay at home today and help your mother?"

Johanna nodded. She wouldn't have gone to school anyway because she couldn't imagine actually saying out loud, *I'm feeling a bit blue today, my grandfather hanged himself.*

"What about me?" asked Florian, but Mom put her hand on his arm and said, "You're going to school. You've got two hours of English class today you can't afford to miss." Florian nodded in resignation. Mom took a sip of coffee, then wiped her lips and looked at Dad.

"Both of your parents committed suicide," Johanna said in a small voice, cautiously, as though she hardly dared to say it. "Don't you think that's strange?"

He shook his head. "No, what for? A whole life has been lived in between."

"All the same," said Johanna. "Maybe one suicide has something to do with the other," and her father snapped at her angrily, "What would you know about it?" And when she asked about what, he said, "About life."

Of course, the Golden Goose is the nicest of the medieval buildings on the square, Johanna thinks. *My parents don't settle for second best.* Two girls are standing ready at the door to take the guests' coats, even though hardly anyone is wearing a coat. It had been too hot for coats all day.

Johanna is standing at the entry to the dining hall. It's a big room. The light, dampened by the broad-crowned chestnut trees behind the building, is softly shining through the windows, which are tall and narrow and make the room look festive. The white balustrades on the raised alcoves—alcoves that look like the upper gallery of an old church—also give that impression, and Johanna thinks, *All that's missing is an organ. Or a curtain that has just gone up to reveal the stage, the last act of the play, the death of the leading man.*

Johanna can just imagine her mother ordering the tables and food for "about fifty to seventy people … there isn't any way to know in advance just how many people will accept the invitation." She can just picture her mother with the owner of the Golden Goose, Mr. Schmeller, going over the menu and selecting the wine. *Prosecco with the first course, red wine for the main course.* She was certain they had discussed the flower arrangements, appropriate to the somber occasion, crystal bowls with boughs from a box-wood tree and white blossoms in between. Roses, more roses, and little flowers with yellow stamens and white, pointed petals that almost look as if they were folded out of paper. She can't remember what kind of flowers they are and is annoyed that she can't recall the name, but she is not going to ask her mother, *no way,* because then Johanna would have to say, "You should've had thistles, why didn't you pick out any thistles?"

Her parents are standing inside the entry, quietly directing the guests to the tables where they're supposed to sit. The tables in the middle are for local dignitaries, the ones farther back are for the employees, including both of the new apprentices, who are wearing embarrassed smiles. They don't know what kind of expression they're supposed to wear at this kind of thing, they hadn't even really gotten to know old Mr. Riemenschneider at all, anyway.

"Please go sit at the table over there on the left, with the relatives," her mother whispers into Johanna's ear, immediately turning to the next guests.

Aunt Amalia, who has grown fat and ponderous in the years since Johanna had last seen her, looks uncomfortable in this environment. She's standing by the door, too, pressing her bag to her chest with her right hand and holding her husband's arm with her left. Uncle Erwin is trying to seem indifferent and unimpressed, but his face is scarlet, and there are beads of sweat on his brow. His black suit fits snugly, and his pant legs are too short so that you can see his striped socks in his freshly shined shoes.

So out of place, Johanna thinks. *So out of place,* and she wants to laugh out loud at how easily a few wrong details can turn a tragedy into a comedy, or at least a tragicomedy. But something wells up in her along the lines of affection for these old, out-of-place relatives, and she softens. "Come on, Aunt Amalia, this way," she says, guiding her aunt—well, really her great-aunt—to the table her mother had pointed out, and she holds out her chair for her.

Aunt Amalia smoothes her skirt over her ample behind before she sits down and presses her bag back to her chest. *That's how she used to press her little black cat to her chest,* Johanna thinks, *before, when she wasn't so fat, when her hair was still gray, not white with all the ridiculous blue highlights. How long has it been?* Johanna recalls her aunt that day, her sorrowful expression. The cat got run over, she was lying by the curb, such a sweet animal, and her aunt's tears were rolling down her cheeks, leaving a thin, shiny ribbon behind. The image is so clear that Johanna bends down and gives her aunt a kiss on the cheek. The old woman turns her head, Johanna feels the soft, pliable flesh sliding over her lips and quickly stands up again, but she doesn't move away. She stands there, her hand on Aunt Amalia's shoulder.

Aunt Irene, on the other side of the table, bends over, the flounces of her blouse falling onto the green-rimmed plate, her pearl necklace swaying in front of her wrinkled neck. She knocks over the artfully folded napkin sitting on the plate to see her sister better and asks why Hubert didn't come. "It's not right, after all, it's his own brother-in-law, for goodness' sake. He should have come."

"Hubert sent a wreath," says Aunt Amalia. "You know perfectly well that he always preferred to live a secluded life, and ever since he went into the nursing home we don't see him at all anymore. Other people still come into town to go shopping, but he never does. Just the other day I asked a woman whether he might have died without our hearing about it, but she said that he was doing fine, he just can't really walk anymore, the poor dear, but what do you expect, he couldn't walk that well before, either, even when he was still young."

She sighs, and Aunt Irene says, "All the same, it was his own brother-in-law."

"Well, you know," Aunt Amalia says with a quick glance to either side, "ever since it happened, the thing with Johanna, they hadn't spoken to each other, you know."

Florian comes in with Mrs. Tschernowski. Johanna catches her mother's searching eyes, takes her hand off Aunt Amalia's shoulder, and heads down the steps, making way for an old man with a cane who she doesn't know, and guides her brother and Mrs. Tschernowski back up to the big table for the relatives. "You sit next to me, Flori. I bet there'll be something good to eat," Johanna whispers, sorry that no other children had come, only old people, so many old people, as though the director had hauled all of the extras out of the nursing home.

I shouldn't have turned down Daniel's offer, Johanna thinks. *Daniel would probably have looked after Florian, why didn't I think of that?* But she couldn't have handled having him here, with her whole family.

Johanna sits between Florian and Aunt Amalia, and from her seat she can see her parents at the big, long table. They're doing the honors, as her mother always puts it, welcoming the guests. You can tell that she's enjoying it, she's in her element. Florian takes a slice of bread, bites into it, and starts to chew. She hears the babble of voices in the room, occasionally her ear can make out a couple of words but without following the conversation. Just like back in April in that café in Jerusalem when the old women had started to speak, when she still didn't know that Mrs. Levin's maiden name had been Heimann, Meta Heimann. Just like she didn't know that Riemenschneider's used to be called Heimann & Compagnie.

Her father stands up, taps his glass, and everyone falls silent. He thanks everyone for all the expressions of sympathy, which are helping him and his family to bear the heavy loss, because it is a loss in every respect, for himself personally and for the public. His father had not merely built up the business, he had played an important role in swaying the fortunes of the city, he had been on the city council for four years, five years on the board of the employers' association. He had spoken early on of the importance of social responsibility, and he had always been a good, fair boss, esteemed and even loved by his employees, and so on and so on.

The people clap, the president of the chamber of commerce and industry stands up, speaks of entrepreneurial spirit. "These are the people who put our country back on the right path after the hard times, their visions for the future are what led us out of the ruins into a new, democratic life, there were too few people like him, a pity, and today there are hardly any more at all, the generation of builders, they were the ones who created Germany's Economic Miracle, the fathers of the prosperity we enjoy today." And Johanna wonders whether his family has any skeletons in the closet, too, because why are they always leaving the details out, about everyone, it's not just her father who does that, and why are they always talking about the hard times as though it were a flood or drought that hit them through no fault of their own?

The first course is served, prosciutto with melon, paired with Prosecco—she just knew it. She isn't hungry and looks around. Fully lit chandeliers hang over the tables, even though it's the middle of the day. The chandeliers remind her of another occasion, *was it his eightieth birthday, seventy-fifth, seventy-eighth? No matter, maybe it went like this every time,* maybe the different memories are melting together in her head into a single memory. They always celebrated birthdays at Johanna's house. All the parties were held at their house, their house was bigger than Grandpa's who, wifeless as he was, had never really managed to settle in comfortably, to say nothing of presentably. "He's turned back into a farmer," her mother had said. The chandelier in their living room, which was brown and beige at the time, had been new, she remembers. Of course, she could ask her mother when she bought the chandelier, that would help her figure out the year, but then she doesn't really care what year it was.

She remembers the polished crystal beads, the crystal prisms, the crystal cones glittering with the light, the glittering filled the room, jumping from the crystals onto the candlesticks, sparkling on the silverware, hopping onto the gold tiepin of her grandfather, it moved with the watch on his wrist when he raised his glass to his friends, it sprayed from his wineglass, from his gold tooth when he laughed, "Thanks, thank you very much, the main thing is that I've got my health, and that's the most important thing at our age, health."

Then most of the guests left, taking much of the sparkle with them, and even in the eyes of her grandfather, who was having one last drink with his friend Friedrich, the glittering disappeared and dampened into a teary glimmer. Their voices lost their festiveness, their good spirits, and turned sentimental when they started reminiscing about the Greek campaign during the war. Suddenly they were just two old men yearning for the Mediterranean sun, white houses, and blue sky, yearning for donkeys loaded with watermelons and for young women with smoldering eyes and cherry lips.

"Why don't we ever go to Greece?" Johanna had asked one time when her parents were talking about where to go on vacation that year. "Everyone says it's so beautiful there, not just the ancient temples but the sea and everything, and even Grandpa says ..."

"That's enough!" her father said, interrupting her with that angry voice that he always used to suppress any protest. "That's enough, I've had it up to here with Greece, you have no idea, end of discussion, we are not going to Greece, ever."

Uncle Friedrich is sitting at her parents' table, across from her mother, his fork trembles when he brings it to his mouth, and he keeps wiping his sleeve over his eyes. He isn't the big shot anymore, since his stroke. Johanna wonders if he still even knows where Greece is, if women with smoldering eyes and cherry lips still mean anything to him, maybe the stroke wiped away all his memories and desires. "Do you remember the village in the mountains, and then that pretty girl with the donkey who brought us water, water in great big earthenware jugs? And how the partisans suddenly showed up ... We didn't have any other options, we had to do it, it was a war, after all, you can't just let something like that go unpunished ..."

Johanna pushes the image of her grandfather aside and turns to Aunt Amalia. "Do you remember your cat that got run over?" she says. "We buried her in a shoebox, we filled the shoebox with sawdust so that she'd lie comfortably, and then we dug a hole under the big elder by the garden fence, and Uncle Erwin put on his Sunday hat and played pastor and gave a grand eulogy, and we cried about the dead cat, Silvia and me."

Aunt Amalia smiles, and her face suddenly looks ten years younger.

"Yes," she says, "she was a sweet animal." And then in astonishment, as though it were a completely new thought, she says, "It was so nice in those days when Klaus was still living with us with his family and you would come visit us during summer vacation. Now they so rarely come out to visit us, sometimes at Christmas, everything has changed."

She turns to her sister and says, "We've grown old, no one needs us anymore, this isn't how we imagined it."

Aunt Irene nods. The servers are clearing away the plates from the first course and are bringing out the tomato bisque. And then the main course, roast saddle of hare with spaetzle and mushrooms, small portions on gigantic plates.

"Can you remember, Irene," Aunt Amalia says, "in those days, the rabbits, we always had to go gather their food from the meadows, dandelion petals, wild carrots, everything, Erhard would always get out of it somehow, he'd always say, 'That's a job for girls.'"

Aunt Irene nods, "But he would slaughter them when Mother told him to, slaughtering, that was a man's job, he never tried to get out of men's work."

"What was he like when he was a kid?" Johanna asks, amazed that she had never asked before. It never occurred to her that he had once been a child, to her he had always been old, and in his youth, the handsome young blond man in the pictures, as though he had been born that way, as though there had been only those two periods of his life.

"He was the brightest boy in the village," says Aunt Irene with pride, "and he was so handsome, all the girls were after him because he was such a looker, so blond and strong, I remember Uschi over at the Old Publican always used to slip me candy so I'd tell her what Erhard was doing at home and if he ever happened to mention her name."

"Oh, he was a bastard," Aunt Amalia says. "He only looked

after himself, and we had to wait on him, he was the oldest. I remember that I used to have to shine his shoes on Sunday mornings, and if I refused he'd box my ears. He definitely had a short temper, you'd have to say, even when he was a boy."

"That's the way all the boys used to be in those days," says Aunt Irene. "It was another time. But that's not true, Amalia. He started acting that way only after he fell in with a bad crowd. I can remember before that, he was quite different. But we shouldn't be talking about all that, not today, it's not proper."

"Oh, stop," says Aunt Amalia. "You always used to idolize him, your big brother, and he didn't treat you the way he treated me or Mother. I took care of her until the day she died, and I could tell you stories about how he used to act, your wonderful brother."

Johanna would have liked to ask what kind of bad crowd he had fallen in with, their brother, Erhard, who she had known only as Grandpa, but Aunt Amalia's face has become reticent, it's clear to Johanna that she cannot ask any more questions right now. *Another time*, she thinks as she considers heading out to the village, she hasn't been there for quite a while, she'll also pay a visit to Uncle Hubert in the nursing home. *Maybe that's the solution,* she thinks, *I'll talk with them, and then I'll know, and that'll be that, that's all I want.*

Before the dessert is served, Friedrich stands up, Friedrich Stamm, he taps on his glass and in a trembling, barely audible voice says, "He was a friend, a real friend, he ..."

And then his voice breaks, he starts to cry, and his daughter pulls him back down onto his seat, waving her hand apologetically, it's embarrassing to her, you can see that. But Mom reaches out her hand over the table to touch Friedrich's arm warmly and reassuringly, saying something that can't be heard all the way back here. Her face has an almost-tender expression. *She gets things like this,* Johanna thinks with pride. *That's what she's good at, understanding, comforting, making the right gesture at the right time, my father is a boor compared to her, he should be glad he found a woman like that, and she looks so good in her black dress and pearl necklace, better than all the other women.* She would have liked to stand up and give her a kiss, but then she thinks, *In a few months I'll be out of here, next year I'll be back in Jerusalem.*

For dessert there is a chocolate mousse with fresh wild berries, and then the last act is finally over and the curtain falls.

Johanna flicks the light on, closes her bedroom door, leans back against the wood, and takes a deep breath. Seven times, seven precisely counted breaths. It's a game, almost a ritual, the same every time, as though returning to a house within a house. And every time she plays this game, she thinks, *What a stupid habit, at least nobody knows about it.* She opens her desk drawer, takes out a sheet of stationery with her name and address embossed on it—her father had had it made for her for her eighteenth birthday—and she picks up the blue ballpoint pen.

But before she sits down, she goes back to the window again, pulls up the shade, and looks out over the houses. Her eyes wander over toward the cemetery that she had always thought, from here, looked like a park around the church, a bit smaller than the city park between Marktplatz and the train station, closer in size to the grounds behind the theater. The moon is almost full. In a few days it'll be round, now it's hanging misshapen in the sky, a dented balloon, just to the left of the tip of the church spire. The river that looks like it's made out of shimmering flecks during the day when the sun's shining on it now looks like a black ribbon, carelessly discarded.

Johanna guesses that her father has probably inherited everything, not only the house on Fischmarkt—which you can't make out from up here in the tangle of all the streets—but also the house on the edge of town that Grandpa had moved back into after he retired from the store, to say nothing of the magnificent old building on Marktplatz that the store is in. Grandpa had held onto it after he retired, so Riemenschneider's had to pay its monthly rent to him, as a kind of pension.

Johanna looks out her window, leaning on the sill. *Everything looks the way it always does,* she thinks, but all the same, something has changed in this view, in this image, as though his grave, invisible in the darkness next to the church, were somehow casting a shadow over its surroundings, as though a fog were rising out of that small patch of earth, weighing over the familiar scene that she had once described in an essay as picturesque. She wonders whether the grave will always be a part of the image in the future, defining this view from her window, even if you can't actually see it.

She leaves the shade open and sits down at her desk. Three days ago they had been sitting around their big dining table, Dad, Mom, and her, writing cards, death announcements. *It is with deep sorrow that we announce the passing of our beloved father, father-in-law, grandfather, and brother.* They had the address lists lying on the table in front of them, Mom had put them together. Johanna soon ran across the Rosenblatts in New York, but the name Levin in Jerusalem wasn't on the first page. She took the second page, quickly scanned the names, but didn't find it there, either. *Where would Mom have gotten the address from, anyway?* She didn't say anything, the name would have upset Dad. "I don't want to hear any more about it," he had said when she had come back from Israel, "I will not have the ramblings of an old woman driving me crazy."

Johanna decided to send a letter to Mrs. Levin herself. She's almost glad to have a reason to write because she has often been writing letters to her in her mind. In Johanna's imagination, Mrs. Levin's contorted face had long since smoothed, the hostile expression vanished, it had softened into friendliness and even affection. In fact, when they had said good-bye Mrs. Levin's face had already started looking quite different—it wasn't just something she was imagining—and her voice had grown quieter and softer, too. Doron's grandmother, Doron's *safta*. Johanna would have really liked to call her *Safta*, too. Whenever she thinks about the old woman, Johanna changes something about the image of her in her head. She isn't playing games, these are necessary changes that she owes this woman, and she's using Mrs. Neuberger as a model for these touch-ups, the wife of the pharmacist on Marktplatz, a delicate, well-mannered lady who must be about the same age as Mrs. Levin, and even looks a bit like her.

Piece by piece over the course of the past few months, Johanna has changed the image. She's painted a warm brown over Mrs. Levin's pale, white skin with big pores, smoothed out both of the sharp folds between her nostrils and mouth, raised the corners of her mouth a bit, returned some youth and vivacity to her lips with a russet lipstick, dusted rouge onto her cheeks, and above all fixed her decaying teeth—which were in urgent need of repair—and slid a bridge into the gap in her upper jaw, which was quite conspicuous when Mrs. Levin spoke. *That's how she would've looked today, like Mrs. Neuberger, if nothing had happened, if she'd remained Meta Heimann, a highly regarded citizen of this city.*

Johanna stares at the empty page, then picks up the pen. *Thursday, September 12, 1995. Dear Mrs. Levin,* she writes.

Dear Mrs. Levin,

My grandfather died, we buried him today. And her hand grows heavy and stiff, refusing to keep writing. It's so quiet, as though she were the only one home, but she knows that her parents are sitting downstairs in the living room with the guests, that Florian is lying in bed in the room below her, presumably he's asleep, too, because she can't hear any music—maybe he just put on his headphones to avoid a fight about it. He was quite pale by the end of the day and didn't want to eat anything else, and when the guests came he said good night and went up the stairs, dragging his feet like an old man. *I've got to talk to him,* Johanna thinks. *I want things to be different for him than they were for me, I'll talk to him soon enough, I'm just not sure when that'll be, but soon enough.*

Laughter is wafting up from the living room on the ground floor where her parents are sitting with their guests, the Bertrams, who arrived only after the funeral, and with Lutz Bauer and his third wife, an architecture student from Brazil who's still very young. *That warm laughter sounds South American,* Johanna thinks. *How is that woman supposed to be sad, anyway, when she doesn't know most of the people in this random town she's landed in? Such a young woman, why did Lutz Bauer marry her, anyway? He's got to be at least twenty years older than her, and she's kind of out of his league.*

Johanna stands up, pushes a CD into the player, Mozart's Piano Concerto no. 27 in B-flat Major, which she's been listening to a lot lately. She happened to hear it on the radio and loved it instantly, sort of like how she fell in love with *My Fair Lady* during the first song or the old songs and skits by Herman van Veen when Daniel was playing her the albums in his parents' collection or songs by BAP. She presses the button, she doesn't want to hear the first movement right now, Allegro, only the second, Larghetto.

Dear Mrs. Levin,

My grandfather killed himself, he hanged himself, without leaving a note. I presume you are happy to hear this news, but it shows that he was not happy. Are you satisfied that he wasn't happy?

Johanna doesn't write these sentences, she just thinks them, her hand is stiff, the blue ink on the white page reminds her of the Israeli flag. *He killed himself*, she thinks. She had been with him just three weeks ago, but she didn't sense what was really wrong with him. Did he know then that he was going to do it, or did he just have one lucid moment, like Dad said, a lucid moment when he realized how he would end up, could she have prevented it if she had been more attentive, and would she have even wanted to prevent it, anyway?

She imagines the headstone in front of her, Johanna Katharina Riemenschneider, the woman whose name she bears. She hears her mother saying, "Your father insisted on naming you that, I wanted to name you Felicitas, the happy girl, but he wanted you to have his mother's name." *Both of my grandparents on my dad's side killed themselves,* she thinks. *Does that mean I'm going to kill myself, too? Can you inherit unhappiness?*

She sets the pen down on the page. She wants to get away, out of this room, this house. She stands up, skips back to the second movement on the CD again, and walks over to the phone. As she dials Daniel's number, she's already thinking about where they can go, Riverside won't work, you can't go out clubbing on the day of a funeral, maybe to the movies or to a café, but really it doesn't matter. She'd be open to any of those things, the main thing is to get out.

"He's not here," Daniel's mother says, "And our sympathies, Johanna. We read about it in the newspaper, what did he die from?"

"He was old, eighty-two, and his health was failing, too," Johanna says, the way her father had told them to answer when people asked.

"He was an old man, eighty-two years old, and his health was failing, too. Nothing about suicide, that's not anyone's business, we don't have to mention that," Dad had said. "When there's a suicide, people start talking, they'd start digging up every little thing, even my mother's death. They'd start asking me questions. That's not what I want, he was old, *finito*."

"It's going to get around," Mom said. "You won't be able to prevent it, things like this just get around," but he just shrugged and said, "Well, then, let people say what they want, the main thing is they leave me alone. He was old, eighty-two, and his health was failing, too."

"Yes, of course, my deepest sympathies again," says Daniel's mother. "No, I don't know where Daniel is, he never tells us what he's up to, he comes and goes as he pleases, as I'm sure you know. Should I leave a message for him?"

"Thanks, that's not necessary," Johanna says, disappointed. She hangs up and goes back over to her desk.

Dear Mrs. Levin,

My grandfather died, we buried him today, next to his wife, Johanna Katharina, who I was named after, she threw herself in front of a train, did you know that actually? Maybe someone told you when you were here a few years ago, when the mayor invited all the former Jewish residents of the city to visit as his guests. I met the Rosenblatts then, but not you, no one mentioned you then, and certainly not seven years ago, in 1988, when the burning question was whether we should have a big celebration for the store's fiftieth anniversary. My grandfather wanted to, but my father was adamantly against it, he was afraid there would be a repetition of the speech he gave at his fortieth birthday.

I didn't understand what the big deal was, but I was curious, which is why I asked Mrs. Müller-Meinert, she had worked for us for a long time. I asked her what my father had meant, and she said, "I don't know if I'm supposed to tell you, but this used to be a Jewish store before." I left it at that, I couldn't understand that, to me Jewish meant belonging to a certain faith, and I thought it was funny that we didn't say our store was Protestant, too. I was only eleven years old at the time.

I forgot about it, but I remembered it again five years ago when the Rosenblatts were in town visiting, they were staying with us, Efraim Rosenblatt from New York and his wife Elisabeth and their daughter, Emily. Mr. Rosenblatt is the son of the people who Grandpa bought the store from, my father explained, which is how they were able to emigrate to America. They were all really friendly, but my little brother and I were sent to bed right after dinner, I don't know if they had a "real talk" with each other after that. But for me it was left at this: My grandfather bought the store from them, which made it possible for them to escape.

You told me something very different, Mrs. Levin.

We talk as little about the former owners of the store as we do about my grandmother. Did you know my grandmother? You must have known her, you fled in 1939, my grandparents were already married then, my father was born in 1953, Johanna Katharina was thirty-eight when she had him, he was the child of old parents, in those days she was apparently extremely old for a first child, "almost like in the Bible," as my aunt Amalia said one time.

I looked it up, she probably meant Abraham and Sarah, who had their son when Sarah was ninety and Abraham a hundred, and Sarah laughed, or was it an angel who laughed? It doesn't matter, in any case I don't think that any angel laughed when my father was born. God promised Abraham abundant descendants, as many as the stars in the sky. But we are not abundant and probably never will be. Johanna Katharina threw herself in front of the train when she was forty-five, my father was only seven years old. I don't know why she did that, in our family people don't talk about things like that, we're a family that doesn't talk about a lot of things.

Johanna grabs the photo album out of the drawer, her photo album. Glued onto the first two pages in front, before the pictures of her as a newborn baby, are the pictures of her grandparents and her parents. There she is, Johanna Katharina, who she inherited not only the name but also the mouth from. She tries to read something on her face, she's tried to do that so many times, but her face remains reticent and distant, despite the smile. The little boy on her lap, who she's actually holding out toward the person taking the picture, is the only person Johanna knows. Underlying the child's face she sees the face of her father, and suddenly it occurs to her that he doesn't only look like his mother, but he's also inherited her smile, the fake smile that doesn't change the reticent expression on his face. *Dear Mrs. Levin, did you hate my grandmother, too?*

Of course she won't write that, maybe she'll just talk with her about it at some point, next year when she goes to Israel right after her graduation exams. She's going to go for a year no matter what her parents stay. She will do it. Maybe she'll work on a kibbutz or volunteer with the Action Reconciliation Service for Peace at an excavation site. No, she'll do the right thing, she'll go to the nursing home, she'll care for old women like Mrs. Levin, women who might have looked like Mrs. Neuberger today if they hadn't had the misfortune of being born Jewish in Germany.

Dear Mrs. Levin ... The phone rings, it's Daniel. "What's up, Johanna, should I come over?" All at once she says she doesn't feel like getting together tonight or going someplace anymore, and she says, "No, it's already pretty late, I'll see you tomorrow at school," and he asks one more time, "What's the matter?" And one more time she says, "Nothing, it was just a bad day, I'll see you tomorrow," and she hangs up.

Dear Mrs. Levin,

My grandfather died, we buried him today, he hanged himself. I wanted you to know.

Yours,

Johanna

She folds the sheet of paper, slides it into the envelope, seals it shut, and writes the address on it, an address she has known by heart ever since Mrs. Levin had written it onto a slip of paper back at the café at the Ticho House, even if this is the first letter she's sending. She thinks, *Please don't have died, Mrs. Levin, I still need you, even if I never really talk to you because I'm too chicken or because you don't want to. I was too late with my grandfather, I should have talked to him a long time ago, but I didn't know it then.*

Too late is a terrible thing to say, Mrs. Levin, please don't have died. Even if you don't know and maybe don't understand, it's important for me to be able to think about you, to know that you're living there in Jerusalem, at the seniors' home in Mishkenot Sha'ananim, not far from the Montefiore Windmill and King David's Tomb and not far from the Armenian Quarter in the Old City, in your small, one-bedroom apartment with a kitchenette, the apartment where Doron must have visited you once a week at least while he was at college there. Oh, Mrs. Levin, you have no idea how many questions I still have, but I'm scared, that's at least one thing I learned when I was in Israel, that I'm not as gutsy and decent as I had thought, my pride has been duly dampened, I have to admit, not only by you, but there was also the thing with Doron. Did you hear about that, or did he even tell you?

Johanna goes over to the window. Before she pulls the shade down, she takes another look outside. Now the moon is impaled on the church spire, its white light pouring over the dome, dripping down from the tower, coating the cemetery and the fresh pile of dirt and all the wreaths and flowers, looking as if someone pulled a white sheet over everything.

Johanna didn't sleep well, she dreamt of Israel. A security officer grabbed her by the arm right after she landed in Tel Aviv, he held the form she was supposed to have filled out on the plane, waving it under her nose, screaming in her face that she was a liar and a cheat. Under the column Father's Name she had written *Robert*, not *Erhard, Erhard Riemenschneider.* She stood there, looking through the glass wall behind the officer and seeing a blue sky and some palm trees. Mostly she wanted to sink down out of shame onto the floor under the curious looks from the other travelers, she could only stutter, "But my father's name really is Robert, Erhard Riemenschneider is my grandfather, you didn't ask for his name at all," and the voice of the officer, who suddenly looked like Doron, grew even louder. "Father or grandfather," he yelled, "it does not matter, it shall be visited upon them to the third and fourth generations," and when Johanna asked, "What?" he answered in the voice of her father: "You don't need to know everything."

"Johanna, wake up," her mother says, shaking her gently by the shoulder. "It's after seven already, did you forget to set your alarm? Hurry up, otherwise you won't make it to school on time, I can drive you if you need."

Johanna glances at the window, her mother has pulled up the shade, and gray light is pouring in, gray light from a gray sky. She pushes her mother's hand away, relieved that she's not really in Israel at the airport.

"I'm sick," she says, and at that moment she actually does feel sick, even though she knows that she's just having a hard time coming back to reality. She stretches out her legs, which are still cramped from the flight and from waiting in such long lines at the counter. Her muscles loosen up in the pleasant warmth under the covers, and she knows she doesn't feel like getting up and going to school, not today. She wants to stay in bed, she loves her bed, she's always loved it, her bed is warm and cozy, in her bed she's protected from curious looks and unpleasant questions, when she's lying in bed nothing can happen to her.

Her mother is worried, "Does it hurt? Maybe you caught a cold yesterday, it would be easy to catch something in this weather, should I bring you something, tea, orange juice, an aspirin? Should I tell Dad that I can't come in to the store today, oh, but there's already so much to do, you can imagine that nothing's gotten done for the past few days, good grief, I really don't know where my head is ..."

As she keeps speaking, she lays her hand on Johanna's forehead, checking, caring, a familiar motion that suddenly touches Johanna so much that she almost says, *Mom, it's not true, I was just faking it, nothing hurts at all, it's just these thoughts, I'm a little confused, stay with me, make everything go away so we can be alone in the house, just you and me, and then we'll talk like we used to sometimes, do you remember when you used to make me chicken soup when I was sick and chamomile tea and ...*

But her mother just keeps talking. "You don't have a fever," she says, and you can hear the relief in her voice. "Maybe it's just exhaustion, everything really has been a bit too much, even for you two. Just stay home, I'll make sure I come home a little early, too bad that Mrs. Maurer isn't coming today, but you can call if you need something."

Johanna nods, lets her mother kiss her, swallows her disappointment, and rolls back toward the wall. She wants to sleep, for a long time and without any dreams, and if she has to dream about Israel then maybe about the beauty of the country, about the Sea of Galilee, for example, which looks so different than it does in the paintings by the old masters, about the shimmering sun over the water, about Tiberias with its seafood restaurants and the ship that sails from its mooring over to the strip of shore on the other side that looks nearly uninhabited, about the mountains painted in every shade, from an amber orange and ochre to a sandy yellow that's almost white. And about the plants that seem to stand apart, even the grass, every tuft of it with broad, pointy blades is an island with its own little mound. And about a shade of green so sere it hardly stands out against the ocher-colored soil, and about the Jordan that she had dreamed of even before her trip.

She remembers how excited she was to finally see this river, the river of rivers, and she imagines it before her, a stream, a trickle that doesn't at all fit its grand name, and next to her Moritz starts laughing, and only now as she thinks back does she understand why, realizing it was just his disappointment that made him react so ridiculously.

She steps away from the group and runs out to the middle of the little wooden bridge. There she leans over the railings, looks into the water, lazily trickling along maybe two meters below her, and she waits for the grand sensation. *Jordan,* she repeats the name, first just to herself, then it whispers its way out of her mouth, the magical word, as though she wanted to hypnotize herself, and suddenly it's there, the grand sensation of having arrived in a world that she had yearned for without knowing anything about it. Tears well up in her eyes, the light is so bright, she isn't wearing her sunglasses, she didn't bring them today—the sunglasses would bug her—she wants to see everything the way it really is, the pure colors, without any brown filter. But the brightness doesn't just affect her eyes, she can feel it on her face, too, on her bare arms, and she thinks it's not just because of the sun, *it's the light that's so different, no wonder this has always been a holy place.*

In a puddle on the shore there's a small, long-legged bird, quiet, motionless, with its head craning forward, one leg pulled up the way she's seen storks do, his feathers are speckled with brown spots, like dapples of sunlight on a wooded path, and insects are buzzing over the water.

She's so wrapped up in the scene that she jumps when Mrs. Fachinger is suddenly standing next to her, saying, "Strange, isn't it, that this trickle of water has played a greater role in our culture than all the great rivers of Europe."

The bird takes flight, Johanna turns to the side, she doesn't want to hear anything. Her teacher's voice is destroying the magic, she should shut up, but it isn't Mrs. Fachinger—it's her mother saying with an emphatic cheerfulness from the door, "I'll bring you up some breakfast." It's a forced cheerfulness, Johanna recognizes the sound, and she thinks, *That's her conscience, she thinks she's a bad mother because she's not staying home to take care of her sick daughter, and actually she's right, I could actually be sick.*

Her mother sets the tray on the desk while she makes space for it on the nightstand. "You shouldn't stay up reading so late," she says, moving the stack of books beside the bed onto the floor. "You're only ruining your eyes."

"Mom, enough already," says Johanna. "I'm eighteen years old, have you forgotten?"

Her mother smiles with a bit of embarrassment. "Sorry, honey," she says. "You're eighteen, and I'm turning into a scatterbrained old woman, don't be angry with me. Just give me a call if you need anything." She sets the tray onto Johanna's nightstand. "There you go," she says, and disappears.

Johanna stays put, alone, but she doesn't feel like any breakfast. She stands up, grabs the pictures she took in Israel out of her desk drawer. *Here it is, the Jordan,* and she's disappointed once again when she contemplates the image. *It looks so insignificant,* she wasn't able to capture the magic of the place, the special light, the mood. She starts browsing through the pictures, and then she has to smile because the next picture is of those little animals that look kind of like long-tailed hamsters.

She discovered the first one by chance, it was lying on a ledge of rock and had nestled itself in the shadows so well that she would never have noticed it if it hadn't suddenly moved, but when her eyes had adjusted to the light she was able to pick out the other ones, too. They were lying by the dozens in the cracks and on the ledges. She stood there all excited like a little kid, just excited, like Florian used to get excited all the time when he discovered a rabbit or a squirrel on walks with Grandpa, and then Grandpa would say, "That's how kids are, when they see an animal they're just happy, trees or stones and all the other things you might see don't matter to them."

The pictures from the Sea of Galilee were the first ones she had taken, although it was her second day in Israel. They had spent the first day in Tel Aviv. They visited Sarah Epstein there in a nursing home, she had been the first girl to study at the Victoria School, but Johanna can hardly remember the woman, she had simply been old, very old, and didn't even have that much to tell them. In 1933 when she was twelve years old she had emigrated with her parents to what was then called Palestine, and the only things she could remember of her hometown and her former school were fragments, individual images that meant something only to her and had no general relevance. And it wasn't just her former home that she couldn't say a lot about, she couldn't say much about her life here in Israel, either.

But everything had been whirling by so fast, too, the flight, the sudden heat, the harsh sun, the confusion, the yelling in a foreign language with all its vowels and guttural sounds. That night they had tumbled exhausted into bed and then drove first thing the next morning to the Nof Ginosar Kibbutz near the Sea of Galilee—that's where they stayed—and that night they were supposed to meet the next alumna, Hanna Bär, who lived in Ayelet Hashahar, another kibbutz in the area.

"We won't have a lot of extra time to see other things," Mrs. Fachinger had said while they were preparing for their class trip. "The country is not particularly large, but we will be meeting eight women. Fortunately, five of them live in Jerusalem or nearby, so we'll be staying there for four days."

At Nof Ginosar, the whole group shared two little one-bedroom houses with kitchenettes, the girls in one, and Mrs. Fachinger and the boys in the other.

The woman who gave them the key spoke English, but she called the rooms *tsimerim,* and Mrs. Fachinger explained that the word is actually related to *Zimmer,* the German word for "room," only with the Hebrew plural ending *-im* tacked on. They thought that was very funny, especially Moritz, who, while they were having lunch in a separate section of the dining hall, kept asking for *breadim, olivim,* and *tomatim* until Kerstin snapped at him to stop if he didn't want get a kick in the *pantsim*.

Right after lunch, a guide took them to Capernaum, which he called Kfar Nahum. He showed them the old synagogue, which Johanna also took a picture of, and told them about the archaeological excavations that were going on all over the country. He said everything in English.

"Old rocks," moaned Moritz in German, who would have preferred to go swimming, and suddenly the guide spoke German, too, saying, "It's true, our country is full of old rocks and new people," and then he continued to speak only in English again. At the end of the tour, he let her take a picture of him, in front of some old rocks and with Moritz.

She looks at her watch. *Just after ten.* She should really be sitting in German class right now. She isn't sick anymore, not a bit. Her bed doesn't seem that cozy anymore, either, and she's hungry, the coffee is cold, but it doesn't matter. "Drink coffee cold and never look old," that's a saying of Mrs. Tschernowski's, and her grandfather always used to answer, "There's no way the two of us could drink enough coffee to look as young and beautiful as my Johanna."

She puts the cup of cold coffee back on the tray, sets the slice of bread with strawberry marmalade back onto the plate, stands up, gets dressed, and goes down to the kitchen. There she brews a nice, fresh, hot, strong cup of coffee and takes it back up to her room. *A free morning*, actually she should really use the time to finally get started on her contribution to the class report, it's high time, she has to turn it in in four weeks and hasn't gotten further than taking a couple of notes. She opens her notebook and grabs a pen.

Every year, the graduating class divides up to work on different group projects, and she had been inspired by the idea of working on the school history project. The group would write articles to be formally published as an annual and distributed later on by the school to the graduating class and official guests. The three previous graduating classes had already created school history annuals, a kind of series, *The Victoria School in Wilhelminian Germany, The Victoria School during the First World War, The Victoria School after 1933.* She imagined it would be quite a bit more interesting than her previous work on the school paper, more interesting and more challenging.

"This year, we will be taking an in-depth look at the destinies of eight women who were previously students at Victoria and who are living in Israel today," Mrs. Fachinger had said. "We will be visiting them, speaking with them, and writing about them. You are all familiar with the annuals that your predecessors created. We will be doing something very special, the life stories of these women."

At that point there were still eight students working on the school history group project, Stefan got sick right after they started and dropped out. All of them were inspired by the topic and set to work on the prewriting stage with zeal. They went through the previous annuals, then they looked at old class pictures, checked out literature about Palestine during the Mandate Period and about the founding of the State of Israel.

Hanna Bär. She really should have decided to do Meta Levin. On their flight home, Mrs. Fachinger was saying that they wanted to do it differently this time, not just write up a list of dates and numbers like they did for the three previous annuals, the eight life stories of these women wouldn't be enough on their own, so, in addition to the report that each group would write together, each group member would also pick one of the women and write a fifteen-page article on her, standard pages, standard margins, 12-point Times Roman, double-spaced.

Mrs. Fachinger had in mind personal impressions, reflections, an article about what the particular woman had experienced and why this or that had happened, and if that was too broad, they could also situate the individual events in a historical context and concentrate more on facts and numbers—but she would prefer a personal perspective. But she hadn't wanted to tell them all about this before the class trip. Otherwise, she thought, they might concentrate too much on the woman that they were each writing about and not have listened closely enough to the other women, too.

"So, each group member will take one woman, and I'll take the woman who's left over. Johanna, why don't you start. Whom do you want?"

She was startled to be addressed directly and lowered her eyes in confusion. An image of Mrs. Levin's face appeared in front of her, at the time she had not yet done any touch-ups to it. Her skin was still white with large pores, her mouth narrow and pale with wrinkles frowning downward, her teeth had brown spots on them, and the space between her upper teeth was clearly visible, but she didn't want to be thinking about this woman, nor the phrase Mrs. Levin had uttered and that Johanna had not been able to let go of since, which is why she quickly said, "Hanna Bär. I'll take Hanna Bär."

She watched Mrs. Fachinger's expression go limp, she had never seen anyone look so disappointed, but the teacher quickly composed herself, and by the time Melanie said that she'd like to write about Meta Levin, Mrs. Fachinger had regained her composure and nodded, "Good, agreed."

"Missed your chance," Moritz muttered from the desk behind her. "Too late." That afternoon when Johanna and Daniel were sitting in their favorite café in the Old City eating ice cream, she told him about it, and Daniel said, "Well, Moritz isn't exactly my favorite guy, but he's not stupid."

She can still remember the conversation clearly, recalling what Daniel had said, it made a lot of sense to her. "The important thing," he had said, "would be to compare the lives that these women have today with the lives that they could have had, I mean of course that would just be hypothetical, just one approach out of lots of possible approaches, and so from the get-go it's just as subjective as the next one, a hundred thousand different things could have happened that would have changed their lives, even if the Jews hadn't been persecuted, but even so I don't think it's enough to write just about what really happened, that's not enough if you guys really want to go into depth with it."

After this conversation, she had felt so confident, and actually she had planned to start her article right away, but things kept coming up and getting in the way, driving lessons, which were so exciting, her birthday, then the test to get her driver's license, then summer vacation, which she had spent at a language school in England, and instead of getting down to work on Hanna Bär she kept writing imaginary letters to Mrs. Levin.

Johanna notices that she's eaten up all the bread and drunk all the coffee, but the page is still as white and empty as before. *Not now,* she thinks. *Not today, I've got the morning off, it would be crazy not to take advantage of it.*

She'll take a walk along the river, maybe a little ways on the path into the woods that goes up to the grand old hunting chalet up on the mountain. She's not sick, she wants to get some exercise, she wants to break a sweat, she wants to run until her legs move on their own and her head is empty and the only thing she can feel is herself, she wants to run until everything else becomes unimportant, until there's only the ground beneath her and the sky above her. And later on she'll lie in the bathtub with lots of bubbles and a CD in her Discman, not the Piano Concerto in B-flat Major but the Nirvana CD that she got from Daniel for her birthday, and she'll forget everything that has to do with Israel, those old women and their stories that go back half a century and that—technically—have nothing to do with her.

And she'll forget everything that has to do with her grandfather who hanged himself without saying good-bye. As though they didn't exist to him anymore.

Day In, Day Out

It's turned to fall, chilly despite the shining sun. Summer is over, the leaves on the chestnut trees along the boulevard look as if they've developed yellow spots overnight, there are still dabs of color, but already signs of withering. It's been four days—no, five—since she's been to this place, but it seems as if it's been weeks, as if it were still summer, late summer maybe, as if the kids at school were still wearing short-sleeve T-shirts, maybe even tank tops, and now suddenly they're wearing jackets, coats, parkas.

She stops at the corner, leans on a fence, buttons up her jacket. It was hot on the bus, and now she's shivering despite the sun, but maybe it's just a shiver from the inside. School kids are passing her by, in groups or alone, but no one is paying any attention to her. Cars are coming around the curve over and over again, stopping briefly in front of the school, letting children climb out. Mothers and fathers who are dropping off their kids and heading on to work.

There, right where the red Peugeot is stopped at the curb, that's where Grandpa had stopped in his Mercedes on her first day of high school, where he had gotten out and opened the door for her, like a lady. She remembers it very clearly, she's thought back on this day more than once, trying to fend off the lethargy that so often overcomes her when she's standing in front of the school. She's been coming to this magnificent old building every day for too long, the Victoria School, erected in the early 1900s as the Academy for Girls, originally for Young Ladies—which she knows from the other annuals on the history of the school—with a curriculum that emphasized home economics. Probably the girls in those days were fed up with school, too, like her, that's probably true for everyone, she just wishes that something different would happen for once. She doesn't want to keep seeing the same people every day, smelling the same meals, hearing the same voices and especially not the regular bells that divide the day up into allegedly easy-to-digest bits of forty-five minutes apiece. Sometimes she feels as though her whole life has been divided up into forty-five-minute chunks, as though the four tones of those bells were chopping up even her dreams.

Standing beside the Peugeot is a well-dressed woman, a lawyer type, in a cashmere jacket, even from here Johanna can tell how gently the material drapes, and she also knows that that type of jacket costs more than a thousand marks. The woman has her arms folded across her chest, her shoulders hunched slightly as though she were cold, but suddenly she laughs, lifts her right arm and waves, the way Grandpa had raised his arm that time and waved. Johanna can't see the child the smile was intended for, there is the usual crowd pushing its way up the stairs to the entrance. The woman lowers her arm, the smile disappears from her face, her eyebrows draw together as though she has suddenly remembered there's an unpleasant appointment awaiting her, she gets back into the car and drives away.

Out of another car climbs a girl in a red coat, still quite little, probably going into fifth grade this year, she hauls out her backpack from the back seat, puts it on, says something through the open car door that Johanna can't hear, and as she runs across the street her ponytail bops back and forth. *That's probably how I used to look*, she thinks, *before the world got so messed up*.

Grandpa had driven her to school on the first day because Mom had to take Florian to his first day of kindergarten. Her brother had been so excited that at breakfast that morning nobody had even mentioned her first day of high school, everything was about Florian, and she had to make an effort to suppress her anger. But then he had come, Grandpa, and picked her up.

She closes her eyes and imagines him standing there, next to his dark blue Mercedes that he was still driving until last year, or was it the car before that, she doesn't know. He always had a dark blue Mercedes. He's wearing a gray suit, a white shirt, and a burgundy tie with the usual gold tiepin, his parade uniform, as he always called it, and of course a hat to protect his bald head from drafts. She suppresses a smile, because that's what she usually dresses him in in her memory, what he most often wore, a gray or blue suit, only his ties had had color, the only color on him. He had only started to dress himself shabbily after he had retired from the store, actually just in the past two years. He smiles, raises his arm, and waves after his granddaughter, the first person in the family to go to a prestigious, college-preparatory high school, he emphasized that over and over again, driving by the Victoria School several times, pointing at the old building and its wide, curved steps with a stone balustrade leading up to the main entry, saying, "You can be proud, you're the first."

His pride was infectious, she had told everyone that she was now going to a college prep, the Victoria School, basking in the ohs and ahs from Mrs. Müller-Meinert in the women's wear department, who she called simply Mrs. Müller in those days, when she was even younger she had called her Auntie Müller. "What a smart girl you are, just like your dad, I think." Johanna picked out new things to wear, *no, no more Mickey Mouse stuff, I'm going to a college prep,* and she smiled, flattered, when the saleswoman said, "Oh, my, my, how time flies." Grandpa had given her a fancy, old-fashioned fountain pen with a gold nib engraved with the initials J.K.R., Johanna Katharina Riemenschneider, in a dark blue case lined with dark blue velvet. Johanna feels a sting as she thinks about that pen, it's still lying in her desk drawer, used only once because no other kid in school had had a fountain pen, she had stowed it in the drawer under the drawing paper, and at some point she had pushed it all the way to the back so she didn't have to see it anymore. *I could use it again now,* she thinks. *Maybe after my graduation exams.*

She opens her eyes, walks a ways, squeezes in between two cars. This is where he had stood and watched her, she had turned around one more time at the gate to the schoolyard to wave at him, then she went up the steps, seven steps, with so many kids who were all bigger than her that she was afraid of being crushed to death. Upstairs in the hallway, Marlene had been standing with her mother, Marlene from her class in elementary school, and she walked over to join them, relieved.

From the schoolyard gate she can see Daniel now, he's standing at the left baluster in front of the steps, his hand resting on top of the round stone cap, waiting for her as always, she should've known. He cranes his neck and waves at her when he sees her, flailing his arms around wildly like a little boy, today for some reason he seems especially young to her, even without comparing him to Doron. He's tall and narrow, and when he stands this way—his weight on one foot, his other knee bent forward, looking as though his leg would flutter in the wind like a ribbon—he always reminds her of the angels on an intricately carved Gothic altar, and reluctantly she admits to herself that he looks good, *and he looks even better when he's naked.*

She walks up to him, which is what she's supposed to do, he's been waiting for her. It's her fault, she could have said, *I don't want you to keep doing this, I don't want anyone to wait for me anymore at all, no waiting, no expectations, I don't want anything anymore, I don't want to see anything, hear anything, say anything. Like you said, leave me in peace, just eight more months and this will all be behind me.* But she didn't say it, she's also not sure whether she would really even want to say it, even if she were braver.

He puts his arm over her shoulder, brushes her neck as if in passing, but he doesn't kiss her because he knows she doesn't like that, she hates public displays of affection, but when she feels the fleeting touch of his fingers on her neck, the weight of his hand on her shoulder, she gets warm. She leans into him, for a second, just for a second, but long enough to think, *Maybe this* is *love, I should stop questioning myself and brooding about things, I should just go with the flow of everything a little more and forget the whole thing with Doron.*

"Was it bad?" he asks. "How're you doing? Did you survive it? I know what it's like, I was twelve when my grandma died, I loved her a lot, she was a great woman, I got along better with her than with my mom, it was just one of those things, I remember how the funeral was, all the relatives were crying, especially my mom, and I couldn't imagine never seeing my grandma again."

He keeps talking and talking, and she knows that he's just

doing it to be nice, he wants to make it easier for her to say something, or not to say anything, he doesn't want there to be any pause where he might sense her disapproval. Things used to be different between them, every morning she used to look forward to seeing his slender shape with his hair that's too long, that he sometimes wears up in a ponytail so he looks like a mix of a choirboy and Karl Lagerfeld.

"It was awful," she says when he stops talking for a second, and she suddenly notices noise in the schoolyard, the sound of children romping around. A ball hits her in the back, she spins around, a red-haired boy grabs the ball, gives her a look that—with a little generosity—she might interpret as apologetic, and runs back.

She lets Daniel pull her into the school, the familiar smell envelops her, a mixture of cleaning fluid and dusty paper, even the sound is familiar to her, the whirl of all the voices, a buzzing like in a beehive, and, when they sound, the four bell tones are as calming as the voice of her dentist, "Don't be afraid, Johanna, just a little drilling, it won't hurt."

Daniel takes his arm off her shoulder as they go up the stairs to the third floor. First thing this morning they've got honors history, of all things. Mrs. Fachinger will be looking at her inquiringly and sympathetically, *she is so understanding it gets on your nerves sometimes,* and Johanna will be reminded of how she ran to the bathroom in that café in Jerusalem, in the Ticho House, where she leaned over the sink and puked.

Suddenly the odor of toilet cleaner and air freshener is filling her nose again, she can feel the hummus and tahini from lunch climbing up from her stomach, the chunks of tomatoes and peppers have sharp edges and cut into her throat. She runs to the bathroom and pukes the memory into the sink, but there aren't any little bits of lettuce, just her normal breakfast, coffee and buttered bread with strawberry jam, nothing else.

She rinses her mouth out with cold water, splashes her face, takes a few squares of toilet paper off the roll in one of the stalls and dries herself off with it. In the mirror her face is pale and strange, she's got circles under her eyes, it's the girl from Jerusalem looking back at her. It's spring, not fall, the summer is still ahead of her, and her grandfather, that goddamned Nazi, is living far away in Germany and has no idea what Mrs. Levin has just said about him and what she has yet to say, or anything about her phrase, "Treasures of wickedness profit nothing."

Daniel is leaning against the window in the hallway outside the bathroom, he's been waiting for her. She's thankful she doesn't have to walk into class alone. It won't be just Mrs. Fachinger in the room, but also the four girls and two boys who went on the trip to Israel. They all noticed it last spring, obviously, everyone notices when a girl suddenly rushes to the bathroom and the teacher runs after her.

One night later on they talked about it, Mrs. Fachinger thought talking would be a good idea. "You can't pretend that nothing's wrong, Johanna. Everyone heard, it's better if we talk about it."

Birgit had tried to make her feel better, saying, "It's not your fault, Johanna. It's not our fault, it was our grandparents'. The blame isn't directed just at you, don't take it so personally."

"That's right," Kerstin had said. "We're not to blame, but I still felt awful when we were at Yad Vashem, at the Holocaust Museum, you guys, too, right? Especially in that cavern where it was pitch black with all the lit candles like stars in the dark, and the names of the one and a half million murdered children were being read out loud on the speakers, with their ages and where they were born, infinitely, one name after another. Honestly, I started to cry in that dark room, and I also wondered what both of my grandfathers actually did when they were young. I felt guilty, even though I didn't do anything myself. I mean, why do I have to feel guilty when I didn't do anything?"

"'The blessing of being born late,'" Moritz said, who always has some famous saying handy when things get serious, which often bugs Johanna, but that time she was happy because his comment had diverted the attention away from her, and suddenly a debate sprang up about German politics, how politicians should treat Israel, and whether and how much Germany shares responsibility for the country that was founded as a result of the persecution of the Jews. It was a heated debate, but Johanna didn't catch any of it, she was in a kind of daze, the voices of the other people swept past her ears like the beating of a startled raven's wings.

Melanie didn't say anything, as usual, nothing that whole evening, she had only laid her hand on Johanna's arm once, seemingly by chance, and as she's remembering it now, Johanna thinks she can feel the pressure of Melanie's fingers on her bare arm.

Suddenly she thinks it was wrong to tell Daniel that no one should come to the funeral, she would have liked to have Melanie there, she wouldn't be feeling so alone with the experience. Melanie wouldn't have said much, but she wouldn't have had to, it would have been enough for her to be there, her composure and natural warmth would have comforted her.

Everyone's there already, Johanna spent too long in the bathroom, class has just begun. Mrs. Fachinger is wearing her beige-and-brown-checkered suit that Johanna knows from the store. It cost eight hundred eighty-nine marks, but it was marked down at the end of the season to five hundred ninety-nine marks, she herself had crossed out the old price the weekend before and written in the new one underneath, she remembers she thought of Mrs. Fachinger at the time, how she would probably be annoyed by the price, but even so there were only three suits left, one size 8 and two size 20s.

Mrs. Fachinger comes to meet Johanna and shakes her hand, mutters something like "My condolences," and then says out loud, "It's nice to have you back, Johanna. We missed you."

Johanna goes over to the empty seat next to Melanie, the taciturn, quiet one, who she's often sat next to since the start of eleventh grade. Not that she's really her friend, not like a best friend when you're younger, now they're much too grown-up for that. Johanna suppresses a smile. She hasn't had a best friend since eighth grade, since Nicole moved away, and then it wasn't cool anymore to have best friends, it was more about cliques, but even that slowly started to wear out, and now all that's left are the people you sit with in honors classes or normal classes, your group project partners, and the occasional couple.

Melanie pushes the chair over to her, smiles, says, "Hi," and takes out her books, smiling one more time. She smells like lily of the valley, her deodorant, a smell that is now very familiar to Johanna. In all the classes they have together, she sits next to Melanie, that's almost like a friendship, even if it's a strange friendship, so restrained that she often forgets Melanie and is surprised the next morning when she sees her again.

They're discussing the Adenauer era after the war, and Daniel is talking about all the old Nazis who stayed in their positions of authority. Hans Globke, for example, was the director of the

Chancellor's Office under Adenauer despite his Nazi past. It was the same story in the business world, and there were judges and doctors who previously had denounced "people unworthy of life," as the Nazis called them, who all stayed in positions of authority after the war, too. "Denazification was just a farce," Daniel says. "Everyone knew it at the time."

Johanna notices that Mrs. Fachinger is looking her way before she answers Daniel.

Johanna can't hear what she's saying anymore. *Denazification,* she thinks. *Was he denazified? I bet, but no one bothered to mention it. I'll ask Uncle Hubert, I'll drive out to the village this weekend. He couldn't stand him, Erhard Riemenschneider. Uncle Hubert will tell me the truth, or at least whatever the truth is to him.* "A humpbacked man, deformed," Aunt Amalia always said about Hubert. "A dwarf." When Johanna met him the last time, she was maybe ten, no more than eleven, and he was barely taller than she was.

Johanna is startled when the bell rings, she hasn't followed anything today in class, time just flew by without her noticing, and she's amazed again at how differently people perceive time, sometimes it's much too short, then unbearably long again. Like the moment before Meta Levin said, "I do not want to have anything to do with that goddamned Nazi." She could read it just from the old woman's expression, she cringed even before she felt the attack, and for a moment she was alone with the old woman in the café, the faces of the older women and her classmates had disappeared, just her and this woman, and she knew something had happened that she didn't understand, at that moment she had stopped being that carefree girl, that sheltered daughter and granddaughter, especially granddaughter.

She gathers her thoughts again, *I've got to snap out of this,* she can't afford the distraction, she needs to do well on her exams, maybe she'll want to major in premed or something, she doesn't know yet, but she doesn't want to ruin her chances, she needs things to work out. Her intelligence has always been adequate for high school—even well suited for its demands—she has never had any real difficulties.

The class periods go by, Johanna functions, she even manages to concentrate for the most part, she answers questions, laughs, if someone makes a funny comment she nods in agreement when the others nod, but she's glad when the day is over.

Daniel is pushing his bike along, next to her, trying to talk her into something, he wants them to get together and do something, "Maybe go to the movies or whatever," he says. "I'll do whatever you want." And she says, "I just want to be alone," and she thinks about her house within a house.

He looks hurt, she knows he means well, he loves her, he's loved her for so long already, and he can't help it that she doesn't love him the way he'd like, or doesn't love him anymore, or whatever. She herself doesn't even know.

"OK, OK," she says. "I'd like to go for a walk, a long, long walk, I want to walk until I'm so tired that I just crash into bed, I want to walk through the woods, maybe jog a ways along the river, if you feel like it ..."

He agrees immediately, although she knows that he doesn't like jogging, or really any sports at all, that's what sets him apart from most of the other boys his age. He's not interested in cars, he likes to read, he likes to have discussions. And he wants to sleep with her, but she quickly pushes that thought out of her mind.

The key is hard to turn, the iron gate squeaks as she pushes on it. She remembers that her grandfather had mentioned a while back that he needed to oil it again, but apparently he hadn't done that, and Johanna wonders how many projects he didn't finish and what all was left undone that might have been important to him before.

She stands at the gate and contemplates the house, which suddenly looks quite different, it looks blind with all the shutters rolled down. The lawn urgently needs mowing, there are weeds growing in the planting beds, even in the cracks between the stones that pave the way to the house, and there are fall leaves lying on the ground everywhere.

She looks up into the apple tree out in the garden that she used to sit under so often, the bench is empty and there are a couple of withered leaves on the table in front of it along with two or three small fallen apples. Everything looks dreary, even the tree looks dreary and old and forlorn—although its apples are gradually getting rosy cheeks. Dreary, as though the house and the yard were also bereaved, or maybe even dead as well, a mortuary, a mausoleum, as though it once had a life that has now vanished—and it's been just two weeks since a crazy old man was living here, worried about his housekeeper, also not that young anymore, who had looked after him for six hours every day.

"What exactly will happen to Mrs. Tschernowski?" she asks her mother, who is helping Florian carry a few nested moving boxes toward the house from the car. She stops, puts down the boxes, wipes the hair out of her face, and looks at the house, as well—confused and surprised, as though she had never seen it before.

"She worked for him for three years," says Johanna. "We can't just let her go, we've got to take care of her."

"Four," says her mother. "It's been four years already, but you don't need to worry, Dad paid her a severance package. And right after the funeral, Friedrich's daughter asked her if she wouldn't come to work for her, she can't manage everything on her own anymore with her father getting so old now." Her mother shrugs, sighs, "Friedrich is getting more and more difficult every day, I don't think he's going to be around for much longer."

She points to the walnut tree right in front of the house, whose expansive crown hides the lawn in its shadow so the grass looks mossy, unkempt, even when it's freshly mowed. "He loved this tree," she says. "Sometimes I think he bought the house just for this tree." She smiles, it's the same compassionate, understanding smile that Johanna has often seen when she or Florian were sick. Sympathetic, understanding, and helpless. "Somehow he never stopped being the poor farmer's boy," she says. "I remember him explaining to me that nuts have a lot of fat and calories in them, and when times are hard you need fat, so nuts can keep you alive, 'Who knows how many people have survived hard times just because they had a nut tree.' Can you imagine, Johanna, he's just bought a house on a gigantic lot, paid a fortune for it, and he's lecturing me about the nutritional value of walnuts ..."

"Here are some lying on the ground now," says Florian, he

goes over, pushes a bit of grass to the side, picks up a nut, and carefully steps on it with his heel back on the path. The cracking is familiar. *It's true, he always used to carefully gather all the fallen nuts,* she had often enough seen him standing under the tree and cracking nuts on a stone.

"Fresh walnuts," Florian says, pulling the yellowish skin off the kernel, he puts it into his mouth. While chewing he asks, "Do you want one, too, Johanna? Should I crack one for you like Grandpa always used to, should I crack one for you, too?" And suddenly she hears the birds and the buzzing of insects. Someone's hammering somewhere in a neighboring house, farther off a dog is barking.

Her mother tears Johanna out of her memories, urging her on, "Let's get going, we don't have time to be lollygagging around here, we've got to finish up today, Mrs. Tschernowski is coming again on Monday for a few days to do the dirty work, but we have to take care of his personal stuff ourselves."

She grabs the boxes and drags them behind her to the front door and without turning around says, "You two should also give a thought to what you want to keep of his things, as a memento ..."

"The rocks," says Florian, throwing a nutshell into the air, it spins back into the grass like a wounded June bug. "I'll take his rock collection, I bet no one else wants it, and anyway he used to take me out collecting all the time, and I want the display case, too, with all the rocks in it. If I scoot the dresser in my room over in front of the window, I'll have a spot for the case."

Johanna looks at him in amazement, it sounds as if he's already thought this through carefully. *Rocks*, she thinks. *Rocks.* And then she says, "Then you have to give me one rock, just one, it doesn't have to be a particularly pretty one, but you have to give me one."

She suddenly remembers Hanna Bär, the woman they had met in the evening at the Ayelet Hashahar Kibbutz in Upper Galilee, who she has to write her article about. She remembers the dispassionate tone, the almost cool voice, that Hanna Bär was telling her story in, about fleeing to Denmark where the Nazis ended up catching her anyway and sending her to the Theresienstadt concentration camp. Only when she talked about the time her tonsils were taken out, in Theresienstadt, did her voice have a different tone—a kind of amazement, as though she still couldn't grasp it even after so long a time. "Can you imagine, I'm in a concentration camp with prisoners dropping dead all around me, and some asinine SS guy who has no inhibitions about killing human beings with his own hands orders that my infected tonsils be taken out."

Hanna Bär survived that horror, but the illegal ship they made it onto, full of the Nazis' victims who all wanted to go to Palestine, was seized by the British, so the refugees were sent to Cyprus and interned. They had to live there in camps again for over two years until the State of Israel was founded in 1948, and then they finally arrived in the Promised Land, which was in no way the Land of Milk and Honey, but a land where a violent war was raging. Hanna Bär was a gaunt woman with snow-white hair cut very short, Johanna had stared at her face—a face in which only the mouth had any expression, as though it had lived its own life—until other faces that Johanna knew from photographs and documentaries displaced Hanna Bär's face—hollow-eyed faces of bodies, emaciated skeletons.

They had sat in the club room of the Ayelet Hashahar Kibbutz, listening intently, their stomachs tightening, to the words of the woman who in those days when all of this happened could hardly have been older than they are now, they had probably all compared their lives to the life of this woman, a life in which there had been no room for what did or did not taste good, only for getting something into your mouth at all, and a life in which it did not matter what clothes you had on. They had been amazed how this woman managed to tell them everything with such indifference. But when they were saying good-bye and Mrs. Fachinger asked whether she could do something for her, her hard shell shattered, and the voice of the old woman trembled when she said, "Go to the Jewish cemetery when you get back home, and set a stone on the grave of my grandparents, Wertheimer—Samuel and Ruth Wertheimer—please, set a stone on their grave and tell them I'm alive …"

Melanie and Moritz went together, they found the grave and set a stone on it, Johanna guesses they took a picture for the annual. She doesn't know anymore how she got out of going with them, although it really should have been her responsibility since she was writing about Hanna Bär, she doesn't remember why she didn't go, either, probably she just didn't feel like doing something with Melanie and Moritz. But now she decides to go there next week for sure. She'll visit the grave of Hanna Bär's grandparents, and the stone that she will set there will be a rock from her grandfather's collection.

Mom has already opened the front door, it's dark and stuffy in the hallway, Johanna has to fight off a sudden attack of lightheadedness when she crosses the threshold, and she thinks, *Maybe it's death that smells like this.* Then Mom rolls up the shutters, flings open the windows, letting in light and air, and Johanna feels better again.

The hallway looks the way it always did, Grandpa's coats and jackets are hanging on the stand as though they were still waiting for him to put them on. Lying on the bureau are two hats, and the woolen cap that he always put on the minute it got a bit chilly outside, *when you're bald you get cold easily, it's easy to grab something or other from the bureau.*

"It goes so quickly," Mom says, opening a box, folding Grandpa's raincoat neatly and laying it inside, "It goes so quickly, the windows have hardly been shut for two weeks, and already it feels like a mausoleum in here."

"What's a mausoleum?" asks Florian, he takes the brown hat off the bureau, puts it on, grins at himself in the mirror, makes faces. Mom must consider that inappropriate because she snaps at him, "Stop goofing around, go into the living room and pack up the rocks, take some newspaper. I think Mrs. Tschernowski set out a stack of old newspapers on the bench in the kitchen."

Florian puts the hat back down, his lower lip pouting, and Johanna thinks, *He gets upset so easily, what is she so annoyed for, he certainly didn't mean anything by it.* "You can pick out a rock for me, Flori," she says to distract him. "Not too big and as round as possible." Florian nods and disappears.

Johanna opens the door to the coat closet and takes out the thick blue sweater that Grandpa had worn so often in the past few years, the collar and cuffs have been worn smooth, a seam has come undone at one shoulder, one elbow has a hole in it, the ripped threads hanging down through it.

"That can't even be given away anymore," her mother says. "Why don't you go grab a big garbage bag out of the dining room for everything we're throwing away. The things that are still good we'll take to the nursing home. Dad already spoke with the director there, they can always use stuff like this."

They work in silence, only once in a while does Johanna hold up a piece of clothing and a pair of shoes and ask what she should do with it. When they finish with the hallway, they move up to his workroom, which he hardly ever used, why should he have, he only ever worked in the yard, he wasn't interested in anything else anymore, and the only thing he read in his later years was the newspaper. When the weather was nice, he would sit on the bench out under the apple tree, when the weather was bad he'd stay in the kitchen.

"Dad wants to keep the armchair," her mother says, and strokes the worn-through, pale-green velvet upholstery almost tenderly, then she traces the picture of a tendril of flowers on the armrest, drawing a shiny, chestnut-colored stripe in the thin layer of dust.

The armchair is very old, you can tell, and suddenly Johanna cautiously asks where he got it. "He didn't have this kind of chair back in his old place. You know what kind of furniture Aunt Amalia and Uncle Erwin have, definitely not something like this."

Her mother shrugs, "No idea, maybe he bought it at an antique shop, but it was already here when I married Dad." And Johanna thinks, *I'll take a picture of this chair when I get a chance and show it to Mrs. Levin. Who knows, maybe it was the armchair that her father used to sit in, or old Mr. Rosenblatt, the father of Efraim Rosenblatt from New York.*

"Do you want the desk?" her mother asks, and Johanna shakes her head.

"But you used to like it so much when you were younger," her mother says, surprised. "You always used to say what a nice desk Grandpa has," and Johanna looks out the window, to the top of the apple tree, and says, "True, when I was younger."

"OK," her mother says. "If you don't want it, I'll have it brought over to Dad's workroom, it really is an especially beautiful and valuable piece," and Johanna decides to take a picture of the desk, too, and of the big oil painting in the living room that shows a dusky moor landscape with so many hues of brown and pink. That painting is also old, the colors have grown a bit darker, in many spots where the paint was applied more thickly there are fine rips that look like netting.

Her mother is lost in thought looking at the tobacco pipes neatly hung in a row on the wall. "Even though he hasn't smoked them for years, these, too," she says. She makes a note on a pad of paper about what is supposed to happen to each thing, and she grabs some newspaper to pack up the pipes.

Then they start on the desk. His papers are lying in the top drawer. "He even kept his old school certificates," Johanna's mother says with amazement. She opens a suitcase retrieved from the attic and starts putting the papers into it, next to the pipes.

"Nothing from the store," Johanna says, looking over Mom's shoulder. "Nothing but old junk, yet nothing from the store," and Mom says, "Dad has all those things in the office, all that's here are Grandpa's personal papers."

"All the same," says Johanna, "it's kind of like he had been a school kid and an old man, and nothing in between."

She crouches in front of the desk, opens the left door, takes an old-fashioned brown money box made of stiff leather from the bottom compartment. The leather has rips in it and is discolored, but the box is still pretty. She flips open the lid, decorated with a stylized tendril of flowers, and discovers a bundle of envelopes inside. All of them are addressed to Mrs. Johanna Riemenschneider, and for a moment she feels as if they were meant for her, but then she sees the dates on the postmarks and realizes these are letters he had written to his wife, to the Johanna Katharina who would later throw herself in front of a train. They're the letters from a soldier on the front, and his wife, Johanna Katharina, had carefully kept them all and put them into this leather purse.

Johanna takes out a letter and starts to read it, and when her mother tries to take the letters out of her hand, she says, "I want these as a memento of him."

"But not these letters," says her mother unhappily. "You could take the collector's cups and saucers from the glass cabinet instead, those are also from your grandmother, why don't you take the collector's cups?"

"Those, too," Johanna says. "The collector's cups and the letters," and it occurs to her that she uttered the words in the same tone that her father uses to suppress any protest. She looks at her mother, confused, "Please, Mom."

After a while her mother nods, "It's OK by me," she says. "But maybe you shouldn't really mention it to your dad, I have no idea how he'll react."

Later on as she's clearing out the closet and cabinets in the bedroom, in his nightstand drawer next to a thermometer and an open bottle of sleeping pills Johanna finds a couple of photographs, snapshots of soldiers in uniform, so blurry that you can't recognize the faces. One photograph is a little bigger and sharper than the others, it shows two soldiers laughing, their arms around two young, black-haired girls. The one soldier is obviously her grandfather, the second one could be Friedrich Stamm. And there's another picture that she already knows from the photo album they keep in the bookcase in the living room at home.

She stares at the tall, blond man in the uniform, you can see the skull insignia and swastika clearly, and suddenly she understands why there are flecks of ink and scraped-off spots on the print of this picture they have in the album at home, it's not because the photograph is so old, as she had always assumed, someone had damaged it on purpose, and she wonders who it might have been, her grandfather or her father.

"We'd best throw these photographs into the trash right away," her mother says. "Your father doesn't need to see them, it'll just upset him."

Johanna puts the photographs into the leather purse with the letters. "Then let him get upset," she says. "I'm not throwing the pictures away. If Dad doesn't want them, that's his problem, I'm keeping them for myself and Florian, it's our right to see the pictures." And she thinks, *Maybe even it's our obligation*, but she doesn't say that out loud, it sounds too pathetic.

Tonight she can't fall asleep, although she's exhausted from the unusual work, all the bending and lifting. It took them the whole day, they piled up the bedding and towels that Mrs. Tschernowski wanted left on the table in the kitchen, sorted the clothes into wearable and unwearable piles, they cleaned out the workshop in the basement, and Florian picked out a drill and a couple of other things that he absolutely wanted to keep, but Mom deemed most of it garbage. *Strange,* Johanna thinks. *Someone dies, and the value of everything that used to belong to him, of everything that he used during his life, changes. Nothing is the way it was, only money stays the same.*

She inherited two hundred fifty thousand marks, an exciting and unsettling notion. They were at the lawyer's office, her parents and her, and he read Grandpa's will out loud to them, along with a listing of the stocks and other assets that Dad inherited. Mom and Dad looked at each other, and Johanna wondered whether it was more than they had expected. But then the lawyer continued reading. "Two hundred fifty thousand marks shall go to each of my grandchildren, Johanna and Florian, from the proceeds from the sale of my house, to be invested by their father in gilt-edged government bonds until their eighteenth birthdays. They shall use the money as the basis for building up their own lives independent from their parents." The lawyer dropped the will onto the desk, awkwardly cleared his throat, took off his eyeglasses, looked directly into Johanna's welling eyes, smiled, and said, "He wrote the will a few years ago, you were fourteen at the time, Johanna, but now you are of majority age, which means that you can avail yourself of the money immediately, but Florian still has to wait a few years."

And she had noticed his swollen eyelids and thought, *He was one of his friends, too, I've seen him before at one of his birthday parties, what do old people think actually when their friends are suddenly not around anymore?* Then the notary had read further, but there weren't any other surprises, the principal heir was her father, his only child.

Only that night when she was talking with her parents back at home did Johanna grasp what it meant to possess so much money of her own, it made her independent, she didn't have to do what her parents said anymore, if she wanted she could take a year off and travel around the world, she could buy a car, she could pursue any dream …

"But it hasn't come to that yet," she had promised Dad that she would not touch the money until after graduation. "You'll still need your diploma," he said. "You've still got your whole life ahead of you, and you'll see that it'll be easier if you start with solid financial footing."

And her mother said, "I would have loved to have a little bit of money when I was your age, then I could have become something more than a saleswoman."

"But then maybe you wouldn't have met Dad," Johanna said, because she couldn't think of anything else.

"That's true," Mom said without smiling. She stood up, poured a glass of wine, raised it, and said, "No matter, that's all history, a toast to my rich daughter." Then she drank the whole glass in one gulp.

Johanna switches on the lamp on her nightstand, stands up, pulls the leather money purse with the letters out of her desk drawer. There are fifteen letters, she doesn't know if that's a lot or not, if he wrote his wife frequently. She starts to read. She can't tell from the letters whether he loved Johanna Katharina, there isn't anything interesting in the letters, just advice about the store, where she might be able to get goods, what tailor she could get orders filled at, that she shouldn't forget to glue the panes of glass tightly into the windows so that they wouldn't pop out from the change in air pressure if a bomb were to fall somewhere nearby, and the blackout curtains, *don't forget the blackout curtains*, and be sure to keep expensive products in the cellar and keep only individual pieces upstairs in the store. Every letter is signed *Your faithful husband, Erhard.* After the fifth letter she gives up, disappointed, stuffs the letters back into the leather box, and hides them in her closet, all the way in back under her winter sweaters.

She doesn't want to have anything to do with it, not with the letters or with the money, at least not for the time being.

It's Daniel coming up the stairs, she knows his gait, his steps sound strangely aggressive because he keeps taking two steps at a time but at irregular intervals. Where she would count the steps to bring them into some kind of pattern, maybe a four-quarter beat, his movements are syncopated.

"So, what's up, why'd you call?" he asks, out of breath, from the doorway, whose frame he fills in his thick blue jacket, and suddenly the room grows bigger and brighter, rays of sunlight shining in at an angle through the window onto the middle of her yellow rug with its mosaic of scattered colors, making them glow.

She is so happy when she sees him that she jumps up and hugs him, and she thinks, *I do need him, this really is sort of like love, I need a person like him so I don't suffocate in this freaking house*, and immediately she corrects this thought, which she finds overly melodramatic, and thinks, *I need him so I don't suffocate from my own thoughts*, and then that strikes her as even more melodramatic.

He pushes her back, looks at her with surprise in his face. She's rarely greeted him this way over the past half year, she knows that herself. Even so, her feelings are hurt by his surprise, she embraces him again almost furiously, so tightly there's no more room between their bodies for anything else, until his warmth passes over to her and the inexplicable, irrational panic that had suddenly gripped her melts away and finally disappears, along with a weird feeling that another person, a stranger, is making herself at home within her, trying to quash the last remnants of the Johanna she had been until April.

She runs her hand over his back, imagining she can feel the individual bones in his spine under the thick, smooth fabric, her hands wander under his jacket to the spot where his small and amazingly round butt starts, and only when she feels how he's responding to her touch does she slide out of the embrace and say, "No, Daniel. Not now."

They both stand there for a moment, hesitant, as though they don't know what they're supposed to do with themselves now that they've stepped apart. Then he takes off his jacket, hangs it on the hook by the door, and goes over to the window where he stands with his back to her. She wonders whether he's just enjoying the view again—"You've got the nicest view that I know of, Johanna"—or whether he wants to show her that her rejection has hurt him.

She contemplates his form in the black T-shirt and black jeans, the contours that stand out, hard against the sunlight, and she wonders why he puts up with her and just takes it when she pushes him away as often as she does. This isn't the first time she's rejected him, the night Grandpa hanged himself was an exception. When they first started seeing each other he would pressure her, almost beg her, but lately he just gives up right away.

She doesn't dare ask him why he's stopped pressuring her, where does his strange devotion come from and what feeds it and what's been keeping it alive for months now already. *Love,* she thinks. *But why does he keep loving me even though I sleep with him so much less often now than before, when I keep him at arm's length so much of the time, why does he accept all my excuses? He's not stupid, surely he must've noticed something changed after I got back from Israel.* That trip has had repercussions for Daniel, too, although she's never mentioned the name Doron to him, but luckily the fling had been so short that even her classmates hadn't noticed.

"Daniel," she says, and he turns around. Suddenly she feels like she's lived this moment many times already, seen him turning around many times before, and she's not sure if she finds it familiar or unsettling, or just boring, but Daniel doesn't give her any time to think.

"OK," he says. "So go ahead, out with it, what is it, why this sudden, urgent need for me to come over?"

She goes over to the desk, takes out the five pages that she wrote about Hanna Bär, holds them out to him, and says, "It's the last sentence, somehow I think I'm starting to lose it, it's making me crazy, I don't even get why."

"The last sentence?"

"Yeah, the last sentence."

The sentence is something that Hanna Bär said, an observation from the time when her name was still Hanna Wertheimer, just before she had been caught by the Nazis in Denmark. She can't remember what Hanna Bär actually said that night in the sparsely furnished club room, but it must have been something along these lines, how else would she have come up with it? She sits down on the bed, leans her back against the wall, and crosses her arms behind her head.

Daniel sits down on her desk chair and reads the sentence out loud, slowly, then one more time: "'She didn't give any thought to what she hoped to gain, nor was it important to do so anymore, because by then every decision was accidental, unpredictable in its results, and therefore meaningless.'"

He puts down the page. "I don't get what you mean," he says. "The sentence is just fine, if it describes everything accurately, you can be happy with it."

"No, no, it's seriously driving me crazy," she says, upset. "I keep reading it and reading it, I'm stuck on it, it's not about Hanna Bär, it's about me, that's what's wrong." And because she recognizes how feeble this sounds, she tries to explain what had been going through her head before he came over. But just as she begins to talk, the panic that had gripped her before takes shape again. "Why doesn't anyone tell us what's important in life?" she begins, shaking. "How the hell are we supposed to find stuff out? Why do people expect us to make decisions when there really isn't anything to decide on, just a chain of events we can't control because they happened so long ago, anyway?"

"You don't need to write a philosophical treatise, Johanna, just your personal opinion about the fate of this woman," he says.

She can tell that he's trying to reassure her but also that he doesn't buy what she's saying, she wants to force him to take her seriously, that's all. "Daniel," she asks, "do you think someone can just go crazy, just like that, completely out of the blue?"

He's taken aback, shrugs helplessly, his lips move as though he wants to say something, but then a shadow falls over his face, and he says only, "Well, I think it's more complicated than that, more gray than blue. What exactly do you want from me?"

Now his voice has that aloof, smug tone she knows so well from school—and that she doesn't like—it tells her that he's avoiding something. *It doesn't matter,* she thinks, resigned. *The main thing is that he's here talking to me, the main thing is I'm getting out of this hole. Let's just play the boy-saves-girl game then, fine by me, maybe it's just his form of revenge.*

"I can't do this," she says, trying to use as aloof a tone as his. "I just can't. Everyone else has turned in their articles, most of them anyway, and I just can't get past these couple of pages, I don't know what to do."

"I told you you should've picked Meta Levin," he says. Going back to the window, he asks with his back to her, "Why *did* you pick Hanna Bär and not Meta Levin?"

"I guess I just didn't trust myself," she says. "I guess it was all too close to me, you know, my parents, people … "

"The whole thing is really pretty whacked," Daniel says. "Eight women who survived the Holocaust and haven't died from old age or whatever else yet. Why aren't you guys writing about men or, even better, about the families? Why just these eight women?"

"Victoria used to be a girls-only school," she says. "And it's not the point, we can't write about everyone, even just naming the 1,504 Jews who were living here in town and in the surrounding villages in 1933 would take up more space than the annual has. And besides, what good would that do? I think it makes sense to focus on one aspect, even if it's so small. It's supposed to be just one tiny stone in the mosaic, we're not writing some kind of history textbook, and, anyway, the students doing the school history group project next year and beyond will still need to have something to write about. I mean, enough already, we've already been over this a thousand times."

Daniel is staring out the window, silent, and she thinks that his shoulders look broader, *I hadn't noticed that before, from the back he's suddenly looking like a man.*

But after a while, when he turns halfway around toward her, she's touched to see how delicate and childlike his profile still is, she thinks that she can see the peach fuzz on his upper lip and chin. But this fondness soon fades because his voice sounds cold as he continues to speak. "Why does your group want to document the lives of people who were so privileged, and only from one single school, just these eight women who are now living in Israel, what about all the others who didn't go to a fancy prep school, there were poor Jews, too, it wasn't just Eastern Europe that had a Jewish working class, Germany had one, too, the rich Jews are a cliché, you know that."

"A lot more Jewish girls went to high school than non-Jewish girls," Johanna says. "At least here. It was over forty percent if you include trade schools and home economics schools. That's an amazingly high percentage."

"And what can we learn from that?" says Daniel in a sarcastic tone, in the voice that always sort of scares her, especially when they're not on the same side. He lifts his index finger and shakes it like an old schoolmarm: "We can learn that the Jewish girls were smarter than the non-Jewish girls. Good job! The old prejudices just won't die. The Jews are crafty and they rip off the honorable but somewhat dim-witted Germans."

"Oh, cut it out," she says angrily. "Don't even start with all that garbage, it just means they worked hard to get an education, for whatever reason. Even for their daughters. That's all."

"I'm sorry," he says, and turns all the way back around, supporting himself on his arms, half sitting on the windowsill. She can't see his face against the bright light outside, but his voice sounds very soft when he says, "This is actually all about something totally different, isn't it? You're not really afraid of making a fool of yourself because your article might not be that good, are you?"

With his sudden softness she finally breaks down and starts to cry. "I'm so sorry that I got involved in all of this," she says, "that I went to Israel at all, the idea was whacked, you're right, and now I can't back out of it, I don't know what to do, I can't just say I don't feel like it anymore. Stefan stopped because he got sick, that's a reason everyone can accept, but I can't find any plausible excuse."

"True," he says. "You can't just get out of it, even the biggest idiot would notice and everyone would be talking about it, that it was just because of your grandfather and the old story, Riemenschneider's is too well known a store, people would start yapping pretty fast, and your grandfather wasn't exactly uncontroversial, either."

She lifts her head, tears running down her face, she tries to wipe them away but then gives up, she doesn't care about looking ugly, everyone looks ugly when they cry. "Do you know that neither my dad nor my mom ever talks about him?" she says. "There's only a picture of him on the bureau with a black ribbon, that's it. He hanged himself and no one talks about it, it's like he's been dead and forgotten for years already ..." She can't continue talking, she rolls onto her stomach and buries her sobs into the pillow.

And then she feels him sit down beside her, his weight pressing the mattress down, she slides into the impression he's made, feels his hip on her side, a warm spot in a landscape of ice, and she sobs even louder when he starts to caress her, evenly, comfortingly, soothingly, the way you pet a dog or a child, and the warm spot spreads, it becomes a soft hole that she drops herself into and sinks deeper and deeper. *Crying is wonderful*, she should have been crying the whole time, *it's calming like a warm bath, and his hands are so pleasant.*

Later on, she doesn't know how long it's been, she's cried herself out, she lies relaxed and feels his hands sliding under her sweater, caressing her bare back, and suddenly she turns around and pulls her sweater up to her neck.

"Close the door," she says, he closes the door, pulls the shade down, and in the sudden twilight her bed turns into a floating, rocking island, she hears the crashing waves, the rising breeze, the hoarse cries of the gulls, when she gives in to him, to his desire and hers, she doesn't know whether she's been caught off guard by her own feelings or whether it's just a longing to finally forget everything, to act as though nothing were wrong, as though she hadn't been to Israel, as though she were still the girl from before, and she doesn't care.

"Three weeks is too long," he whispers in a hoarse gull's voice, and she says, "Yeah, three weeks is too long, much too long."

Long after Daniel leaves, she's still lying on the bed rocking and thinking, *Strange that I always have to think about the ocean when I'm having sex,* but maybe it's not that strange, it's just because she was at the ocean the first time she slept with a boy, two years ago, at summer camp in Brittany.

She knows that her mother will be calling her down to dinner soon, she'll stand up and go downstairs, she'll sit at the table and act like nothing special is going on, she'll listen to the conversation about the store, who called in sick again, who accused who of what, she will learn, with an attentive expression, how the new line of suits is going to look, she'll nod when Mom says, "Mrs. Neuberger was in today, the wife of the pharmacist, she bought a new coat, the sage one with the red lining and the button placket over the zipper, the coat that I liked so much, too, really a lovely piece, but actually she's a bit too old for something like that," and Johanna will imagine how Mrs. Levin would look in a coat like that, and she'll nod when Florian says, "Can you read over my essay after dinner, Johanna?" And she'll smile, touched, when she sees the relief in his expression and she'll think, *My little brother, I should take better care of him*, and she'll remember how often he used to beg to sleep next to her because he was afraid of nightmares. She'll be the dutiful daughter and sister, the granddaughter of old Riemenschneider, you remember him, from Riemenschneider's in town on Marktplatz, she can hold out for a couple more months.

She thinks about Daniel and really has no idea why she doesn't sleep with him more often, maybe she just wants to punish herself for cheating on him with Doron, even if it's hard for her to think of it as cheating exactly, and somehow she's furious at Daniel that he didn't come on the trip to Israel, that he didn't protect her from Doron.

And then she notes to herself that she didn't tell him anything about the money, as though it were unpleasant for her to have inherited it, and she remembers Meta Levin, how she said, "Treasures of wickedness profit nothing."

You're mistaken, Mrs. Levin. There's quite a bit of profit.

 Only grudgingly did Mom give Johanna the keys to the car when she asked at breakfast if she could have the car to drive up to Aunt Amalia's. "What do you want go up there for?" she asked. "You haven't visited them in so long. Why now all of a sudden ..."

"I promised her when she was here for the funeral," Johanna said. "Besides, I've got to get out of here for once, I need a little change of pace. And why shouldn't I drive up there, when I was little you were always glad to send me there so someone could look after me during vacation, you never had time, have you forgotten?"

"Oh stop, it wasn't that bad," her mother said, but it was only a halfhearted protest, her voice a little hesitant. Johanna knew she'd won immediately, it was so easy to give her a guilt trip, and then her father stepped in and said, "Oh, let her go, after all she's not a kid anymore, you can't keep setting rules for her, and besides she can buy her own car now if you won't lend her yours."

"But we agreed she would leave the money in her account until after graduation," her mother protested. "She did agree to leave the money alone."

Her father shrugged, "*Agreed*," he said. "Who cares if she agreed? It's her account. She can use it whenever she wants."

As she had predicted, her mother gave in right away. "Well, I don't need the car today, anyway," she said, her relief audible, but then she took her revenge by asking, "Florian, maybe you'd like to go along?"

Johanna was startled, but luckily—even before something ill considered could slip out—Florian said he couldn't because he has soccer practice today. "We're playing Gutenberg in two weeks, it's a really important game, so I can't skip practice today." Johanna was so thankful that she volunteered to study English with him that night.

She's already out on the road in the countryside, the stress of city driving is easing up, she's driving fast, enjoying it as the fields and meadows race past her. She has a sense of freedom when she's out driving, even though she knows how absurd that sounds, *freedom,* when you're locked in a tin box. *Still …* , she thinks, smiling at the thought of the car her parents promised her for graduation. And if they renege, she can just buy one.

She's looking forward to seeing Aunt Amalia and imagines her surprised face as she mulls over which questions she'll ask her, what she really wants to find out. He was her brother, he must have been someone different, before, before he was Johanna's grandfather, when he was still living in the village, in the impoverished conditions they're always mentioning. And she'll also visit her uncle Hubert, Hubert Keller, the brother of Johanna Katharina Riemenschneider, née Keller.

Johanna recalls Aunt Amalia's house, Grandpa's parents' house, being rather small, *a little run-down,* she thinks now, even though this would never have occurred to her as a child. She had always enjoyed going there, especially because of Silvia and Thomas, who were about the same age as her, she was envious that they had a dog, their own dog, and that no one set rules for them and that they could do whatever they pleased, during vacation at least. No one ever said, "Change your clothes, you can't go outside like that" or "Watch what you're doing, what will other people say?" And they could make noise, as much as they wanted, with all the noise from the carpenter's shop that Uncle Klaus ran, the incessant sawing, hammering, drilling, you didn't even notice. The door to the shop was always open, and when Johanna would run past, she always paused a moment to breathe in the wonderful smell of fresh wood and sawdust, a smell that also enveloped Uncle Klaus when he came into the kitchen for lunch.

To the right in front of her a farmstead comes into view, off in the distance she can see horses out in the field and she slows down. It's a riding center, next to the house she can see stables, in front of them is the riding ring where there are a couple of cavalletti lying around, on the straight part of the course at the back there are three fairly low fence hurdles. A woman is leading a horse out of the stable, a black horse that must be pretty young, he's skipping restlessly on legs that are still too long. The woman tightens the reins, she pats the horse's neck and turns toward a man who is repairing a post-and-rail fence, she apparently yells something at him, then he puts the hammer aside, raises his arm, and waves.

Maybe I should drive over to Martin's and go for a ride, she thinks and suddenly feels as if nothing is more important than sitting on a horse, feeling the warm body, hearing the rhythm of the hooves on the soft trails in the woods.

Of course, maybe he won't let me take a horse out at all, she muses. She hasn't been there in ages, two years or more, although she used to spend the majority of her free time there, at Martin's Equestrian Center. Only when she finally realized she would never ever be good enough to win a tournament did she lose interest, and Grandpa, who often drove her to her riding lessons, had made no attempt to hide his disappointment. "I would really reconsider if I were you," he had said. "You haven't even won a third-place ribbon for yourself yet." And even now, here in the car, driving out to the village where he had spent his childhood and youth, his comment still hurts her feelings. She stopped riding and started jogging, there aren't any competitions for jogging, you're just alone with yourself and don't have to prove anything to anyone. *But riding is something completely different,* she thinks. *I could've just said I don't want to do tournaments anymore, I just want to ride.*

Suddenly she has the scent of horses in her mouth, but she knows she's only imagining it, the car windows are closed and, besides, the horses are too far away. And then she notices she's tensing her thighs as though she wants to put pressure on a horse's sides. She laughs, to herself, but her muscles don't relax until after all the horses have passed from view. *If the weather stays like this, maybe I'll drive out to the riding center tomorrow, and if Martin says something stupid, I'll just leave again.* What harm can it do, her grandfather is dead, and it's not as if anyone will even ask her why if she decides to stop going.

The house he grew up in is on the edge of the village, in the distance Johanna can just make out her aunt and uncle working in the garden. Aunt Amalia is deadheading the flowers and ripping the withered stems of the annuals out of the ground, a pile of yard waste shows she must have been working for a long time already. Uncle Erwin is raking up the fallen leaves under the chestnut tree. *The chestnut tree,* she thinks, and shakes her head surprised. *I'd almost forgotten the chestnut tree*, and she notices the swing that hangs on a thick, almost perfectly horizontal branch, she'd almost forgotten it, too. She had really loved swinging on it, high, higher, so high that the meadow and house disappeared and all she could see was the sky above her, and then suddenly the roof would come back into view, the house, the door, the meadow, and then the meadow, the door, the house, the sky, again and again, and Aunt Amalia's voice, "Hold on tight, really tight, OK, so you don't fall off!"

Aunt Amalia stands up when Johanna closes the car door. She brushes the hair off her forehead, wipes her hands on her apron before she holds them up to shield her eyes from the sunlight so she can see, and she looks so pleased, the way Johanna had hoped, then she runs with outstretched hands toward her. "Erwin!" she calls. "Never mind the leaves, Johanna is here," and to Johanna she says, "It's so nice of you to come out and visit us, I can't believe it. Come, child, I'll put on some coffee, and I'll send Erwin to run and get a couple things at the baker's, maybe some puff pastries. I remember that puff pastries used to be your favorite."

Johanna waves her hand and says, "I'm not hungry, Aunt Amalia," but her aunt insists on coffee and a little something to go with it, and when they're sitting in the warm kitchen, which has hardly changed other than the microwave and new electric range—and actually the kitchen still looks a little run-down, too—Johanna notices that she is in fact a little hungry, and the pastries taste so sweet and gooey the way she remembers, and she licks her sticky fingers off the way she used to.

She lets them ask all their questions, tells them about school, Florian, "Yes, he's doing well at school," why didn't she mention that he's just been moved ahead a grade, she should be sure to look after him a bit more in the future, he can't help it if his mother has so little time. "Yes, everything's OK with us, yes, Mom and Dad are good, the business is doing fine, even with all the new boutiques and jeans stores and the like, we have our regular customers, you know how it is, the upper-class types …" She gives a forced laugh, "We've had to adapt, of course, five years ago we did another renovation and expanded the product lines, downstairs we've also got a new lingerie section. Riemenschneider's still has a good reputation, and—," she adds, so that she can finally get to the subject she's interested in, "we have a lot to thank Grandpa for."

"Well," says Aunt Amalia, returning her partially eaten pastry to the plate. "Yes, that's certainly one way to put it." The friendliness drains from her face, her mouth narrows.

"He always worked hard, nothing was handed to him on a platter," Johanna says, a sentence that she had heard other people say so many times before.

She watches her aunt's lips move, her thick fingers clench into fists, her fingernails turn so white you can see the bits of dirt under them even more clearly than before. "*Worked hard,*" she says angrily. "He forgot a long time ago what hard work really is, he was always wearing his fancy suit when he'd stop by, suit and tie and hat, that's not how you look when you work hard, but that's how he always was, he always used to …"

She's huffing angrily, surprising Johanna, who wonders where all the anger is coming from. Aunt Amalia's face turns red, even the skin on her arms under her rolled-up sleeves develops red spots, she pounds her hands a couple of times on the dinner plate, in a restrained way, as though it were impossible for her to really vent her rage.

"Calm down, Amalia, he's dead," Uncle Erwin says and lays

his chapped, calloused hand on her forearm, a weathered, brown-freckled hand, so heavy it presses into her aunt's soft flesh, making indentations as though her skin were the smooth surface of some vanilla pudding. Johanna can't take her eyes off her aunt's arm, off the indentations under Uncle Erwin's fingers.

"She's upset just because he acted so shabbily toward the family," Uncle Erwin tells Johanna. "All he ever did was take advantage of everyone. We were good enough for him after his wife died, and he could always send his son out here to us, and later on you, too, but when our son was having trouble he didn't give Klaus one penny, we had to sell the fields to pay his debts. We were just small-time farmers, we didn't have anything, and Klaus was earning a good living with his carpenter's shop, he was a good worker, he worked hard, but his debts just got to be too much for him."

"When was that?" Johanna asks.

"Oh, fall of 1988," Uncle Erwin says, and Johanna calculates that that was the last time she had spent vacation out in the village with Florian, when she was eleven. "That's why we stopped coming out to visit," Johanna says, surprised and depressed. "I didn't know, no one told us anything about it."

"You were just a child," he says. "Why should they have told you anything?"

"But I didn't ask, either," says Johanna. "I just accepted it. I can't remember if anyone talked about it at all, about why they stopped sending us out to visit, at the time I just thought it was because Uncle Klaus had moved away with his family."

"And why did he move away?" says Aunt Amalia, starting to weep. "Only because he couldn't stay here anymore, that's why he left, and that's why we're so alone now that we're old, and if it weren't for your dad, we would have had to move away, too, we could never have looked anyone in the face ..."

"Your dad helped us out a little," Uncle Erwin says. "It was a secret, the store hadn't been fully signed over to him yet, but it didn't matter in the end. The carpenter's shop went belly-up, but at least we were able to pay the debts that our Klaus owed private individuals."

Johanna stretches out her hands and lays them over the fists of her aunt and feels her relaxing slowly, her fingers loosening up again. "If your grandma had still been alive," she says, taking a tissue out of her apron pocket and blowing her nose, "if your grandma had still been alive, everything would have been different, she was a good woman, she would never have left us in the lurch. God only knows what he did to her that she had to do what she did, but to outsiders he always played the gentleman, he was certainly good at that."

"Stop it, Amalia," says Uncle Erwin. "He's dead, and we should leave the dead in peace," and Aunt Amalia forces a smile and says, "Yes, you're right," and to Johanna she says, "Oh, I should have kept my mouth shut, none of this is your fault."

Johanna bends forward and rests her face on her aunt's old hands, which smell like earth and icing. She can't ask any more questions, what was he like when he was a kid, who were his friends, how did he get involved with the Nazis, how did he talk about Jews? *Next time*, she thinks, and kisses Aunt Amalia's hands. "I'm so sorry, Aunt Amalia," she says softly. "Do you guys need anything? Can I do something for you?" And she thinks about the money that she has inherited, it would be only just to give some of it to her grandfather's sister and her husband.

But Aunt Amalia shakes her head. "We have everything we

need," she says. "Just come visit us once in a while, it does an old lady good to know she hasn't been completely forgotten." There aren't any accusations in her voice anymore, she sounds soft, and for a moment Johanna feels little again, like the child she used to be.

"I'll come out again," she says as she says good-bye. "I'll most definitely come out to see you again." She hugs her aunt, who smells of sweat and soil, a smell that she knows well, that's how her grandfather also used to smell when he would work in the garden.

Before she climbs back into the car, she lets Uncle Erwin explain the route to the nursing home to her. He waves to her as she pulls away, but Aunt Amalia stands in the doorway, her arms at her sides, looking exhausted. Johanna regrets upsetting the old woman so much with her visit.

The Workers' Welfare Association Nursing Home is a renovated mill with a modern interior, the old building is still covered with grapevines whose leaves are already turning fall colors. The building is in a valley at least two kilometers outside the village. She knows the valley, this is where she used to go mushroom picking with Aunt Amalia, and when she parks the car in the lot next to the building, she thinks, surprised, *It's so beautiful here, I never noticed it before, when I was a kid*. She looks up at the tree-covered slopes, among the pines there are a few beeches and oaks, the edges of the treetops glow yellow and orange, and somewhere off in the distance a woodpecker is tapping out his hard, fast rhythm. Johanna bends over, picks up a crimson grape leaf, looks it over, and drops it again.

A nurse shows her the way to Uncle Hubert's room, on the second floor of the old mill. The stairs are steep, *fairly dangerous for old people*, she thinks, even though they had tried to make them safer with rubber edging. An old woman is coming down the stairs but stops and scrutinizes her curiously. Johanna says an embarrassed hello when she passes her.

She hesitates in front of the door, it's been so long since she's seen Uncle Hubert, the last time he was still living with his wife next to the church in a little house whose kitchen was the only room she remembered. She had never visited him of her own accord before, only if Aunt Amalia asked her to. He used to scare her a little with his humpback and his much-too-large head on his twisted shoulders, she was afraid of him, also of his wife with her strange tics, always saying things Johanna didn't understand, and not just because of her garbled pronunciation, and she never seemed to remember who Johanna was. Johanna always thought she was a witch, *that's how witches look.* Now, in front of Uncle Hubert's door, she realizes his wife must have had cerebral palsy. *Kids can be so cruel. But no one ever explained to me why they were both so different.*

She knocks and then opens the door when a surprisingly powerful voice calls, "Come in!" The room is small and crammed full of furniture, and despite the open window it smells a bit stuffy, of dust and household cleaners and the sickeningly sweet smell of pipe tobacco, which she recognizes from her grandfather.

The old man is sitting in a wheelchair by the window, which is low enough for him to look out, now he turns his big head toward her. "Hello, Uncle Hubert," she says. "I'm Johanna, Johanna Riemenschneider, do you remember me?"

"Come closer," he says with his powerful voice, which doesn't at all seem to match his frail body. "Come closer, I don't see that well anymore."

She goes toward him and has to bend over to give him her

hand. He shakes it for a long time, and she stands, still bent over in front of him, looking down at him, uncertain because she doesn't know whether or not she should crouch down so their faces are at the same level, and he's pressing her hand as though he wants to fight the shaking of his own hands. *His eyes are clouded like a blind person's,* she thinks, but he's not blind. He's looking at her intently, then he smiles, the smile flies over his face, changes it, this is how he used to look when Aunt Amalia would push her into the somewhat gloomy kitchen, and again she thinks, *Kids can be so cruel.*

"Johanna," he says, "I recognize you. You look like your mother, only your mouth is from your grandmother. Pull up a chair and sit with me."

She pulls a chair over to the window and sits down opposite him. She notices his hands, which don't ever stop shaking, and she recalls what Aunt Amalia had said at the funeral, that no one sees him anymore, and she asks out of sudden inspiration, "Uncle Hubert, I brought the car out here today. Do you maybe want to go for a drive?"

He beams, but then suddenly his face falls. "Not today," he says. "The nurse is coming early today, even before dinner, to give me my injections, she wants to leave a bit early today for the weekend, I'm sure you understand."

"Maybe another time?" she asks, and he says, "On a Sunday, that would be nice, you know, I would love to drive up to the hunting chalet in the mountains, if the weather's nice, I would love to see everything one more time."

"Good," she says quickly, and grabs his hands to stop the shaking. "I can't tomorrow, but next Sunday I'll pick you up and we'll drive up to the chalet, is three o'clock good for you?"

He nods. "I'm sorry I can't offer you any coffee, we were

 served coffee early today, at two, and I drank it all up already, I didn't know I would be having a visitor today."

He says it in such a ceremonious tone that she realizes he hardly ever gets visitors, if at all.

"That's all right, I've already had coffee this afternoon," she says. "I was over at Aunt Amalia's. She says hello, by the way."

He nods but doesn't respond to Aunt Amalia's greeting. "How old are you now?" he asks, "How long has it been since we've seen each other?"

"I'm eighteen," she says, "and I was eleven when I was here during vacation the last time."

He pensively rocks his head, which is also shaking, though not as much as his hands. "That's quite a while, then," he says. "Two years after that my wife died, and I moved here into the mill. What else could I have done? I can hardly walk anymore." He points to two crutches leaning on the windowsill. "I can still manage a bit with those, I sit in the wheelchair only because it's easier for them to take me down to the dining room." He shrugs, a movement that distorts his twisted body even more.

"Are things going all right for you here?" she asks. "Do you need anything? Can I do anything for you?" And again she thinks about the money.

He shakes his head, "No, no," he says. "I can't complain. Things are just fine here. I get everything I need, which is more than I could expect." He looks at her curiously. "And you?" he asks. "Why have you come, now that Erhard has died?"

She's speechless for a moment, she has the feeling of being looked through, but then she collects herself, obviously he would be able to tell that her visit has something to do with the death of her grandfather, after all, she hasn't visited him in so many years. She tells him about her trip to Israel, of her encounter with Meta Heimann, whose name is now Meta Levin, a condensed, matter-of-fact version of the story, and she asks if he can tell her anything about that era, she knows so little and no one else wants to talk with her about it. "What did my grandfather do?" she asks. "What was my grandmother like, did her death have anything to do with the old story? What about the others, what about you, what did you do?"

"Oh, they didn't want me," he says bitterly. "I mean, just look at me. I was at no risk of becoming a Nazi. After the war I was just fine with that, glad and thankful that I was never put in the position of doing something I would later regret. During the war I worked in the factory, and after it was bombed out I got a job at the post office. I was at most a tacit supporter of the Nazis because I kept my mouth shut, but nothing else."

Then he talks about her grandfather, about his enthusiasm for the Nazi movement, he was one of the first ones, he joined the party long before thirty-three, "you should have seen him, raising his arm high, strutting around in his uniform, how loud he would roar 'Heil Hitler!'"

He takes his hands out of hers, jerks up his right arm grotesquely. "Like this," he says. "Like this." And she thinks, *A caricature worse than any other,* and she no longer has any idea why she was so afraid of Uncle Hubert when she was little. She's ashamed to look him in the eyes.

But then he lowers his arm and continues speaking. "Your grandmother had a Jewish friend in school, I think. Your grandmother liked her, she was the daughter of the cattle dealer."

"Don't tell me she secretly helped her flee," Johanna says, suddenly exasperated. "It's like everyone had their own personal Jew that they saved, to show off how humane they really were in their heart. I don't believe stories like that anymore."

He shakes his head and smiles. "Don't worry, I won't try to put one over on you, but she was a good woman, my sister Johanna. I never heard her say anything bad about Jews until she started dating that Nazi. He was very handsome, strapping, if you know what I mean, he could have had any girl he wanted. I remember clearly how she said she didn't understand why a man like that would give her a second look at all. We were poor, you can't imagine how poor we were, we had nothing. Erhard Riemenschneider was a good catch, the Riemenschneiders at least had their own little house and a few fields." He rubs his dry eyes and continues, "But he didn't bring her any happiness. She was at first, of course, she was content back then. She never said anything against the party, and I'm sure she was OK with the store your grandfather finagled for himself with the party's help, otherwise he could never have pulled it off, no one could have."

"I know," Johanna says. "*No man truly gets rich behind the plow.*"

"She was a good woman," he continues. "I can't say anything bad about her, and she had it rough with him, and then it took her so long to have a child, that really took its toll, she was thirty-eight when she had your father, no one was expecting it anymore. But even that couldn't save her, the child, she was so young when she killed herself."

"Do you know why?" Johanna asks.

"No," he says. "No one knows. People used to talk about it, everyone wagging their tongues, and I've racked my brains, but I just don't know. At the time he was having an affair with a salesgirl, people were saying, but I can't imagine that that was the reason, that salesgirl was certainly not the first, your grandfather wasn't the type to stay put."

He rubs his twisted shoulder with his hand, his head is now shaking more noticeably as he continues speaking. "Sometimes I think it didn't have anything to do with him at all, why she killed herself, look at me, we are not a healthy family, it could be that we are also sick on the inside. My wife and I, we didn't have any children, we didn't want any, either. You met her, she was also handicapped, who would have taken me otherwise? We were unlucky in life."

His voice breaks, but he regains his composure. "But you, you're healthy," he says. "You've inherited only her mouth and her brown eyes, otherwise you don't resemble her at all, and you're also much taller, much taller. And so slim. You're prettier than she was, she had a good heart, but she was no beauty. To be honest, I also wondered why Erhard married such a girl, and one without any money, to boot."

He lifts his head, looks at Johanna. "I'm so glad that you've come. The first time that someone from your family has visited me since I've been in the mill. Your mother always sends money and packages on Christmas and birthdays, and she also came to my wife's funeral. Your grandfather didn't come, your father, either. Just her, she's a good woman." His voice grows softer again, the words are fading, she can hardly understand him anymore, talking has obviously exhausted him.

She stands up. "I've got to get going," she says, "but next Sunday I'll stop by again, then we'll drive out to the chalet."

He nods, "Yes, there's more I can tell you, but I'm just too tired now, I'm not healthy anymore, you know." He gives a bit of a laugh, "I've never been healthy, why should I be healthy as an old man, then?"

She kisses his cheek, strokes his shaking hands one more time. At the door she turns around and wants to say something nice to him, for example, how sorry she is that she didn't visit before, that she's ashamed, not for her grandfather but for herself, but he's sitting with his head slumped over onto his chest, he looks like he's asleep. So she just pulls the door quietly shut behind her.

She strolls down the narrow street to the Old City with Daniel, it's such a nice day, one of those fall days when the memory of the past summer covers the world again like a silken scarf before the first storms blow it away, the sky is clear and its blue so light that the thin strips of clouds fade into it like steam. Johanna loves this light, it's so different than on summer days, so much softer and more ethereal.

And because today is so nice, she also said yes to Daniel immediately when he suggested after school they finally go on the walk they had planned to take to look at some of the buildings where the eight women had lived as children. She called home to let them know, her mother wasn't back from work yet, but Mrs. Maurer promised to tell her. Then they got a copy of the old map of the city from Mrs. Fachinger, with the houses of former Jewish residents marked with Stars of David. The map is from the very early twentieth century, lots of the street names have changed, previous green spaces now have buildings on them, and many of today's suburbs were still their own, outlying villages then, separated from the city by fields and meadows.

"Fortunately, it shows the river and the churches so we can orient ourselves,"

Daniel says, "and a couple of the place names have stayed the same, too."

Passing behind St. Catherine's Church on Fischmarkt, Johanna looks back at the building that now belongs to her father, an old-fashioned, two-story building that's now rented out to an insurance agent. Then at the site of the old dye works, they turn onto what appropriately used to be called Färbergasse, which is now called Lindengasse. The buildings are as narrow as the street, and a bit crooked, leaning against each other as though they needed each other's support. They're old, you can tell, but carefully renovated with half-timbering and windows framed in ornamental scrollwork, both painted dark brown. This area has gotten expensive, in part because of the central location, in part also because of the quiet, the streets here are so narrow and winding that they are closed to through traffic.

They walk around a bend and come somewhat abruptly into a square in the middle of which grows the age-old linden tree that has given the street its name. Its leaves are just starting to turn yellow, but many of them have fallen off already, the tree's crown looks a bit thin and tattered, it hangs out so far that the branches seem to be touching the second-floor windowpanes on both sides of the street. In the summer when its leaves grow in, the tree is impressive, but even now it dominates the square.

House No. 7 is where Schoschana Rappaport used to live, whose name is now Susanne Klein. Today a lawyer has his offices here, the brass plate with his name on it is gleaming in the sun. Johanna takes off her backpack and puts it on the bench next to Daniel under the linden tree. A few sparrows are hopping around in front of them in the fallen leaves.

She doesn't try to evade Daniel's arm as he drops it around

her shoulder, it's so peaceful here, as though they were in another town, in another time. The traffic is zooming through streets not far from them, but here it sounds like nothing more than a steady rushing. The loudest sound here is the chirping of the sparrows, and in one of the houses someone's playing piano. *Hits from the twenties*, Johanna thinks, *how fitting, as though Daniel and she had paid extra for the music.*

"Too bad I don't have my camera," she says. "The light is so beautiful, I could have taken pictures for the annual, I'll come back here in a few days with the camera, maybe I could send a picture to Schoschana Rappaport, too."

"I don't think she'll recognize the house," Daniel says. "This used to be a poor part of town when they were living here, a really poor neighborhood, the buildings were renovated only in the past few years, I can still remember watching them haul plaster away out of one of the buildings and exposing its half-timbering. So, what is Schoschana Rappaport like, actually?"

"Fabulous," Johanna says, straightening up, "she's simply fabulous—garish and brash, so brash you don't know if you should clap enthusiastically or turn away so she can't tell what you're thinking. She lives in Jerusalem with her son and his family, and she speaks German in this amazingly thick dialect, as though she had never traveled farther than the next town her whole life." Johanna leans back again and giggles, both amused and touched as she describes the woman, who did in fact look as if she had never been farther than the next town, heavy and big-breasted, with carefully combed wavy gray hair that you might have thought was a wig, but a woman like her would never wear a wig. Johanna instantly knew that when she saw Mrs. Rappaport in the café at the Ticho House, which is where they had met with the women over coffee, five of them at once, because Ruth and Mira Weiss—the two sisters—had also come to Jerusalem from their kibbutz nearby. They looked the way you imagine pioneers in the desert, thickset with brown hair and tanned faces.

Before that, they had explored the Old City of Jerusalem, they walked through the narrow streets, inspired and fascinated, they were amazed at the little shops selling spices, textiles, silver, souvenirs, and quite a lot of religious kitsch, especially on the Via Dolorosa, which they had imagined quite differently, with more consequence and grandeur, but instead it was one religious-trinket store after the other. Dominik had bought votive candles and a rosary made of carved olive pits for his grandmother, and the others bought presents, too, and Johanna was sad that no one in her family was religious. A little boy with beautiful almond eyes and black curls tugged on her arm, and he pulled a handful of coins out of his pocket and said in English, "Very old, very antique, very cheap." She bought a couple of coins from him and later gave them to Florian.

They had walked the whole length of the Via Dolorosa up to the Church of the Holy Sepulcher, and Johanna was surprised that Melanie knew all fourteen stations of the cross by heart. Between the tall buildings it was pleasantly cool, and only when they were standing on the Temple Mount in the blazing sun had they noticed once again how hot it was in Jerusalem. And how beautiful. Johanna would never forget how deeply moved she was by the beauty and splendor of this city, a city full of contradictions, full of contrasts, where poverty and wealth, old and new, religious and secular were so interwoven you had the sense you were wandering through time and across continents, every stone, every building seemed to have a historical significance, everything was "very old, very antique," and full of life.

After the din and crowds of the Old City, the park surrounding the Ticho House was a relief. They had actually planned to visit the museum, which, as Mrs. Fachinger said, has an especially impressive collection of menorahs, but they were late, and they didn't have enough time, the women were probably already there.

Most of the guests were sitting at tables in front of the café, the interior space was almost empty, apart from the five waiting alumnae. Johanna still remembers clearly how hesitantly and uncertainly they had gone in, how they shivered in the cool room after being out in the heat. "Air conditioning," Moritz said behind her. "All the air in Israel is air-conditioned, that can't be healthy, if you ask me." She hadn't answered him—she had noticed Schoschana Rappaport and couldn't take her eyes off her.

The woman was sitting at the end of the tables that had been pushed together, and she looked so inappropriate, so out of place. *The wrong woman in the wrong place,* she'd thought, and right after that, *There is no right place for a woman like that, she would look out of place anywhere.* She was sitting under a window, her dark skirt had slid up tight over her thick knees so you could see the beginnings of her fat thighs. Everything on her bulged, her hands that she had folded over her fat stomach, her fingers, her bare arms protruding from her short-sleeved blouse. She was wearing jewelry, rings, earrings, and heavy chains, everything was too big and too showy to be real, and she was wearing makeup, way too much, too thick and too garish, the powder was too white, the lipstick too red and smeared on her upper lip, and her eyebrows had been plucked into thin arcs, which Johanna was familiar with only from old photos of movie stars. *Ridiculous*, she had thought. *Why does she do herself up like that, doesn't she have anyone to tell her?*

But later when the woman started to speak, there wasn't anything ridiculous about her anymore, despite her thick dialect. Johanna forgot the smeared lipstick and the plucked eyebrows, she didn't see the layer of powder anymore, she heard only the longing in the woman's voice, she saw only the pain in her beautiful dark eyes.

"The woods," she said when asked about her memories of Germany. "I've forgotten everything else, and I don't want to think about it anyway, but I would love to go for a walk one more time in the woods, I'd like to see the trees, smell the moss, hear the birds. I yearn for the dim twilight, the sunlight angling through the leaves, and at night I dream that I'm touching the trunks of trees that are cool and moist from dew, I dream of the little white woodruff flowers and autumn crocuses, white anemones, lilies of the valley, and tiny, white wild garlic blossoms, the older I get, the greater my longing. Have you seen what people call the woods here in Israel? It's individual trees with tiny crowns, a paltry line of plants, and the scent is paltry, too, just like the green, there is no real green in this country, I feel so sorry for my children and grandchildren who have no idea what I'm talking about. Sometimes I go back in a dream through the woods, and when I wake up and see the eucalyptus tree in front of my window I want to cry because I've woken up. I know that I should be glad to have a eucalyptus tree in front of my window, but the truth is it always reminds me of the woods of my childhood and only intensifies my longing, and when I see a chameleon, I think of squirrels. And the spring, I'm sure you've seen the hot spring in the woods up around the beautiful old hunting chalet, or maybe it doesn't exist anymore."

"Yes, it does," Johanna said. "The hot spring's still there, they groomed the spot again last year, and now there are benches up there," and she thought of Grandpa, who also liked to roam through the woods looking for mushrooms and picking wild berries and always bringing home some new rock for his collection, but never, ever did he talk about the woods with such a longing fondness.

She wanted to say something comforting but didn't know how she should phrase it, but then Mrs. Rappaport kept talking. "But don't think for a minute I long for Germany," she said, and her voice now sounded hard and aggressive. "I don't want to have anything more to do with that country, not with the city, not with the people, I will never go to Germany again, it's just the woods I miss ..." Her lips, covered too thickly in lipstick, trembled a little, she pressed them together, and Johanna knew there was nothing she could have said because there was no way to comfort this woman.

"So, who's writing about her?" Daniel asks. "Who picked her?"

"Dominik," Johanna says. "You'd hardly believe it, but he responded to her really enthusiastically, Dominik of all people, who otherwise only ever thinks about clothes, he spent the whole evening sitting beside her, idolizing her, as though she were Madonna in the flesh. I'm excited to see how his article turns out."

"'A Treatise on Woodlands and Their Impact on the Psychology of Human Beings,'" Daniel jokes. "I bet he's taking a psychological approach. How did she get out of Germany?"

"She had an easier time than the others," Johanna says. "She had one brother and one sister who were a lot older than her, from their father's first marriage, they emigrated to Palestine in thirty-three and later sent her an immigration certificate, permission from the British to immigrate to Palestine. She was still a kid, which is why it worked, but not for her mother, she was later deported along with others and murdered in the camps."

"And her father?"

"He had already died before all that. She said, '*Baruch Hashem*, he was lucky, everyone who died early on was lucky.'"

They sit in silence for a while, then Daniel stands up and says, "Come on, let's go over to Gerbergasse, that's where two of the women used to live, Hanna Bär and Josefa Brenner. You haven't told me anything about Josefa Brenner."

Johanna stands up reluctantly and picks up her backpack. *It's so nice here under the tree, which I suppose Schoschana Rappaport could see from her window when she was little, the way she sees the eucalyptus tree now when she looks out her window in Jerusalem. Schoschana Rappaport, who thinks about German squirrels when she sees an Israeli chameleon.*

On the way, she tells Daniel about Josefa Brenner, who has a completely different story. She went to Israel by way of South America, only after the founding of the State of Israel. "She's also a Victoria alumna," she says, "but she was born in Poland and didn't come here until she was six years old, and her family continued on to South America right after the Nazis took power, I think to Bolivia. Germany was just a stop along the way for them."

"And who picked her?"

"Tanja."

"Of course, I should've known," he says disparagingly. "Tanja, our little class globe-trotter," and Johanna doesn't respond.

A lot of Jews used to live on Gerbergasse, named for a tannery that once stood there, the map labels each of the Jewish houses with a Star of David, and a hundred meters ahead, there, where the parking lot is now, that's where the synagogue used to be before "Kristallnacht," but the only sign of the synagogue today is a historical marker on the wall at the back of the lot. The house that Mrs. Bär lived in was apparently bombed out during the war, and in its place a one-story narrow box of a house was put up instead, something temporary that looks older and more run-down than the *really* old neighboring buildings with their pointed gabled roofs.

"Did Hanna Bär come back when the city hosted that event for its former Jewish residents a few years ago?" Daniel asks. "Too bad we were still too little to really be interested in that back then."

Johanna shakes her head. "No, she's never been back since she fled Germany. She said she would have liked to come, but her husband was against it, he swore he would never set foot in 'that damned country' again, and she didn't want to come without him."

"Did you guys meet him?"

"No, he didn't want to see us, that night he even went over to a friend's house so he could avoid having to see us even by accident, he would have preferred for her not to have had us over at all, she said. We've got to understand, she said, his experience was much worse than hers, he's from Poland."

She turns her head, looks over Daniel's shoulder to the parking lot and back to the neglected one-story house. "When Hanna would go to the synagogue, which isn't here anymore, she left from this spot, from her house, which isn't here anymore, walking with her parents and brothers and sisters, who aren't here anymore," Johanna realizes. "And here on the street is where she would have played with her Jewish friends, certainly with Josefa Brenner. Nearby there was a kosher butcher's shop, and behind Fischmarkt with its fishermen's stalls there was the Jewish nursery school and the Jewish elementary school that she went to ... Wow, it's been sixty, seventy years, and without this map you would have no idea that any Jews used to live here, there's nothing left here to remind us of them, nothing other than the historical marker for the synagogue."

"Yeah," Daniel agrees. "And no one talks about it, and even if someone did, it would probably just sound like when people say, 'the Celts once lived here, they've found graves that prove that Celts used to live here.'"

"Graves," says Johanna, suddenly remembering the rock from her grandfather's collection that she's been carrying around with her the whole time. "I need to go to the Jewish cemetery, I owe a favor to Hanna Bär, do you want to come?"

She has often walked past the high cemetery wall, but until now she's never been inside. The gate is locked, a sign says that you can get the key from the pharmacy across the street.

"So, you want to get into the Jewish cemetery," the pharmacist asks, adding suspiciously, "I have to take down your names and addresses, you never know, even if you don't look like people who would desecrate a cemetery."

There are two keys, one is big and heavy and opens the wrought-iron gate, the other is for the secondary padlock. The gate has been well oiled and doesn't squeak when they open it. They stop a moment, surprised, the cemetery feels strangely isolated, a desert island, not just because of its high walls but also because of the tall trees and all of the bushes, they feel almost like archaeologists who have made an unexpected discovery.

The graves look old, they're overgrown with weeds, many of the headstones have been tipped over, a few are already so badly weathered that you can no longer read their inscriptions, and still others have sunk down into the earth, only fragments are still sticking out. Many of the headstones bear two inscriptions, on one side the names of the dead are in roman letters, on the other, in Hebrew.

They walk through the rows. "Here. Wertheimer—Samuel and Ruth Wertheimer," Johanna says, and then they're standing in front of the grave. She takes off her backpack, takes the stone out, and sets it on the headstone next to a big pebble already there, Moritz and Melanie probably laid it there when they were here taking pictures.

Daniel looks around. Some of the headstones have stones on them, others don't. "What does it mean, actually, when Jews set stones on graves?" he asks.

"Mrs. Fachinger explained the tradition is originally from when people wanted to prevent wild animals from digging up graves," she says, "so you put the stones on the grave to protect it, but today it's a symbol of remembrance, you do it to show that the dead person isn't forgotten."

"Wow … there are a lot of graves here without stones," Daniel notes, and Johanna says, "Well, where are the stones going to come from if the dead people's descendants were either killed or don't live here anymore?"

They look around and Johanna realizes that he's thinking the same thing she is. She puts her backpack back on, they leave the cemetery in silence and then run almost as far as the park behind the theater to see if they can find suitable stones there. Daniel packs them into the pockets of his jacket, Johanna fills her backpack, then they run back. At each grave that doesn't have a memorial stone, they read the names of the dead out loud—at least the ones in roman letters that are still legible—and then set a rock on the headstone. Then Johanna discovers the grave of Meta Levin's grandparents—Moritz Heimann, who founded Heimann & Compagnie, as she now knows, and his wife Rosa, both died on January 18, 1940. As Daniel moves on to some other headstones, Johanna lingers here, setting two stones onto the grave, and thinking, *This one is from your granddaughter, and this one is from your great-grandson Doron, who has never seen your grave and probably never will. He's in medical school in Jerusalem.* Then she turns and follows Daniel, who has stopped in front of a magnificent old stone tablet to try to decipher the inscription, which is much too badly weathered.

A lot of the names show up again and again, Wertheimer, for instance, Heimann and Weiss, too, they must have been big families. And each time Johanna notices that someone died after 1933 and before "Kristallnacht," she thinks, *That person was lucky, everyone who died early on was lucky.* They also find the headstone of Ruben Klein, Schoschana Rappaport's father, Died on May 17, 1937, May He Rest in Peace. "The hands," Johanna says, pointing to the image carved into the headstone. "Can you see the stylized blessing hands over the inscription? They mean he was a Kohen, a descendant of the priestly class."

They set the stones they have left over on children's graves, then they carefully close the gate behind them and take the key back. "You spent a long time in the cemetery," the pharmacist says, suspiciously. "Perhaps you were engaging in an extracurricular activity behind the headstones?" He chuckles at his own joke. Johanna and Daniel don't answer him and get out of the pharmacy as fast as possible. They walk in silence side by side, and when they turn onto a big street, Johanna feels as if she's returned home from a long trip.

Daniel is the first to say something. "Don't start thinking we've made up for anything," he says. "The Jews have been forgotten and they'll stay forgotten. We were basically just playing a game, and a childish one at that, we shouldn't be proud of acting like children, saying 'kissy, kissy, all better,' like some happy ending to a Mother Goose rhyme, and thinking everything's all made up for now," and she suddenly imagines Mother Goose goose-stepping to "Sieg Heil!" salutes, but she doesn't share the image with Daniel to avoid starting something.

"I'm not proud," she says. "But I'm glad we did it."

They keep walking. When they reach the square in front of the train station, Daniel carefully asks, "Do you still want to come over to my house?" And she touches his hand lightly and says, "Yes, very much," even though she isn't entirely sure that she does, maybe she'd rather go home and crawl into her bed. But suddenly she feels so close to him again, like when things were going really well, she couldn't bear to disappoint him. "Very much," she says. *Very much.*

Johanna's father pounds on the coffee table so hard that his half-full glass tips over, the wine running over the dessert plate, painting a glistening red stripe over the varnished brown surface. Her father winces, tilts his knee to the side, but it's too late, some has dripped onto him, there is a spot on his gray slacks. The wine is dripping onto the floor, Johanna can't turn her eyes away, compulsively she starts counting the drops until Mom jumps up, runs out, and returns with a kitchen towel, and starts to wipe—frantically, as though she could avert a looming catastrophe with her wiping and rubbing if only she were fast enough.

Johanna stays seated, defiant, enraged. *Why is she doing that?* she thinks. *He was the one who tipped the glass over,* but then she sees her mother's face, her open mouth, her lips quivering as though she wanted to say something or as though she were waiting for someone else to say something. As her mother walks past the television nonchalantly to turn it off, Johanna thinks, *She's just stalling for time, Mom doesn't know where it's going to go from here, whose side she'll take.* Maybe she was only buying time to think what to do, but Johanna actually takes her mother's behavior as a sign of encouragement, an exhortation to keep talking. Suddenly it's so quiet in the room that you can hear the ticking of the old clock on the wall, which used to hang in her grandfather's living room, the engraved brass pendulum on the long wooden staff is moving rhythmically back and forth—another object that she will take a picture of.

Florian stands up, mumbles something about an essay that he has to finish for tomorrow, says good night, and hurries out of the room. No one stops him, and for a moment Johanna is tempted to follow him, they are both used to evading arguments with their father. But she suppresses the urge, it isn't courage that keeps her here, but defiance, sheer defiance.

Her father wipes off his slacks, the dark spot on his thigh is fanning out. It's so round and dark red, like in the crime shows he likes to watch on TV, that Johanna instinctively looks for the bullet hole, even though she knows it's just red wine.

She doesn't understand how this all happened, it was a normal evening, they sat down in the living room after dinner with their dessert, walnut ice cream, switched on the TV to see the news. The anchor was reporting on a former member of the SS who may no longer be competent to stand trial because of his poor health, and Johanna said without thinking that that can't happen to Grandpa anymore, and then her father clenched his fist and pounded the table.

After Florian leaves the room, her father says quietly, but in a voice that does not disguise the anger he is suppressing, "You just won't give up, will you? You're just hell-bent on waking sleeping dogs, you're just as stubborn as him. So, what do you want?"

She musters all of her courage and says, "He *was* a Nazi, what did he actually do? You've got to know, you must have asked him sometime."

She expects him to react angrily, but he doesn't. "Yes," he

sighs. "He was a Nazi, that's the way it is, there's no way to sugar-coat it, he was a party member, and that's why the Americans sent him to prison after the war. He was held for half a year, he paid for it." He hesitates, and then he says, "I would've liked to have a father who wasn't a Nazi, too, but it's not something that can be changed, hindsight is easier than foresight, you weren't alive during those times. Can you be so certain how you would have acted in those days?"

True, she thinks while he pulls a tissue out of his pants pocket and busies himself with the wine stain some more, *who can be so sure what they'd do,* and she remembers the controversial comment about the "blessing of being born late" that people attribute to Helmut Kohl. According to Mrs. Fachinger, it actually originated from Günter Gaus, who was the director of the Chancellor's Office under Kohl. Kohl said it only in Israel. But then Johanna says out loud, "Even if you don't know what you would have done yourself, it doesn't change the fact that he was a Nazi, and even if you didn't experience it yourself, you have to be allowed to form your own opinion—"

He interrupts her, throwing the tissue onto the coffee table. "So you think you're in a position to pass judgment? Don't be so damned smug, you've got no right to play the judge here. So your grandfather was a Nazi, so what? You're going to have to live with it, you can spend every day wishing it weren't so, but you can't change it, you can't turn back time. You can't undo anything, and I mean not one thing, and now he's dead, can't you at least let him rest in peace?"

Johanna watches Mom stand up again, take the dirty plates with the uneaten ice cream into the kitchen, and return with a bag of Parmesan breadsticks and a bowl, the bag rustles as she pours the snack into the bowl and then she sets it out on the table, maybe just as a distraction to ease the tension, maybe also to show them that she's still here even if she's not saying anything.

Johanna turns back to her father. "What did he do?" she asks. "Do you know what he really did in the war?"

"What do you think, he was on the front," her father answers. "He wasn't a concentration camp guard, if that's what you mean, he was a simple private on the front, he hadn't been assigned to an SS Einsatzgruppe yet, he spent too long avoiding the military for that. That's what he said, anyway, when I asked him. He had the store after all, for him it was all about the store, or so he said."

Johanna decides to have a breadstick after all, she chews it slowly while she considers how to formulate her next question so that he doesn't get as upset as when she told him about Mrs. Levin when she got back from Israel. Slowly she says, "Mrs. Levin said her parents had been rich, really rich, but that Grandpa cheated them, and all they got was breadcrumbs."

He draws his eyebrows together and pushes out his chin. "Mrs. Levin," he says, and his voice gets louder again, "Mrs. Levin is an old woman, and what she says is crazy talk, the ramblings of an old woman who doesn't know what she's saying anymore."

His tone gives Johanna goose bumps, she would have preferred to get up and run away, what business of hers is all this anyway, but she knows that if she doesn't ask now she'll never dare to again, and then she'll never find out what really happened, and what Mrs. Levin said really will become nothing but the ramblings of an old woman. *I'm doing this for you, Mrs. Levin,* she thinks. *I'm doing this for you so you won't be left a rambling old woman.* She looks at her father, fights against her desire to just give up and go to bed. "So what *was* the deal with the store?" she asks. "Surely you must know."

"He bought it," her father said. "For the building on Marktplatz that the store is in, he paid a hundred ten thousand reichsmarks, which was the currency in use at the time, and then he paid another twenty thousand for the property on Tuchwebergasse, so a hundred thirty thousand all together, that was a lot of money in those days, in 1938, and the store wasn't worth very much anymore at that point, it had been completely run down. You tell your Mrs. Levin that they weren't rich anymore, the Heimanns and the Rosenblatts, they should have been happy he bought them out, otherwise they would have had to leave Germany without a penny. Mr. Rosenblatt said that as well, he was happy that my father bought it instead of someone else, he said, his son told me that when he was here, and your Mrs. Levin should be grateful, instead of stirring up trouble between a child and her own parents and grandparents, you tell her that. And, later on after the war, when they took him to court, the big-shot heirs of the original owners, he paid them even more. I don't know how much it was, the court set the amount, it must have been quite a chunk of change because he had to sell the house on Tuchwebergasse, that's when we had to move into the garret over the store. In any case, in 1938 he paid them a hundred thirty thousand reichsmarks total, for a run-down store and a run-down house, he didn't steal it, he paid for everything."

"Where did he get so much money from?" Johanna asked. "He wasn't a rich man, you guys always said he worked himself up 'with the labor of his own hands,' I mean you don't just suddenly have a hundred thirty thousand marks lying around as though you were going to go out and buy a piece of furniture or something."

He straightens up, sitting tall in the armchair. “What, is this some kind of cross-examination?” he says. “He took out mortgages, loans for himself and for his wife. His sister Irene and her husband cosigned the loan as guarantors, he went into debt over his head, but he paid off everything down to the last penny. It was a lot of money for a run-down store, he did them a favor.”

Now he’s said that sentence twice, Johanna thinks, but she’d never heard the part about him being taken to court after the war. “So, what was the deal with them taking him to court, the heirs of the original owners?” she asks. “What was that about?”

Her father takes a sip of wine, puts the glass back down carefully, and wipes his hand over his lips before he answers. “They went to court saying he had robbed them, they wanted to drag his name through the mud, which is why he agreed to settle and pay rather than continue to fight them.”

“When was that?” Johanna asks. “Were you born already, do you remember?”

She sees his face turning red and doesn’t understand why he’s getting so angry at this particular question after he has been giving her answers to her other questions so calmly, but she can tell that she’s gone too far, she shouldn’t have asked this question. And in fact he starts to yell, “What do you want to know that for, why are you digging around in these old stories? And don’t act so full of yourself, you’ve always lived very well off the store, am I wrong? You’ve always gotten everything you ever wanted. And now you’ve inherited a quarter million to boot, what eighteen-year-old has a bank account as padded as that?” He clenches his fist again, but he softens his punch to the tabletop this time, the glass merely trembles without falling over. “Enough of this, I don’t want to hear anything else about this, I don’t need to justify myself to you, you're just a spoiled brat showing off her intellect."

Johanna stands up, leaves the room, and slams the door behind her, she's furious and hurt, she takes her coat and storms out of the house, out into the rain. She can hear the front door opening again behind her and her mother calling after her, but she doesn't turn around, she doesn't ask if she can take the car, she runs down the street, she wants to go to Daniel's house, she has to talk to someone who doesn't have anything to do with all this.

The rain is pounding against her face, it's running through her hair into her eyes, but she doesn't wipe it away, she runs down the street half-blind, she's shivering the way she shivered in the Ticho House, where the room was cold compared to the heat outside. Suddenly she sees it all in front of her, the five women, her classmates, Mrs. Fachinger, how they're sitting there, each of them with a coffee or an orange juice in front of them, some with a slice of cake. The delicate, well-mannered lady speaking right now is Meta Levin, née Meta Heimann. She's talking about her childhood, her parents, her books, and her violin—especially her violin—and how she'd dreamed of becoming a famous soloist, but then nothing turned out the way she'd expected it to.

"My parents were well-off," she says. "More than that, they were rich. Until Hitler came along I wanted for nothing. We owned the largest clothing store in town, Heimann & Compagnie, on Marktplatz, an ideal location, today it's called Riemenschneider's ..."

It's suddenly quiet, everyone is looking at Johanna.

She's surprised, she's never heard the word Heimann before, she's only ever heard of the Rosenblatts in New York, who visited her parents when the mayor had invited them to town for that event, but she vaguely remembers someone once mentioned *two* Jewish families when everyone was talking about the original owners. Why hadn't anyone mentioned this Mrs. Levin, née Heimann, before?

"Did you visit the store when you were in Germany?" Johanna asks. "Did you talk to Mr. Riemenschneider?"

And then the woman utters a sentence that Johanna will never forget: "No, I do not want to have anything to do with that goddamned Nazi."

Everyone looks at Johanna again but they turn back around quickly and pretend that they hadn't heard the sentence. Johanna's dazed, she feels as if her childhood has come to an end at this moment, gone forever, or maybe it never existed. A happy, sheltered childhood—even if she comes to believe later on that there is no such thing as a happy, sheltered childhood—not for her, not for lots of other people, it's an illusion, people have talked her into it, the happy childhood, *you've got it good, you want for nothing, you're neither hungry nor cold, you can have anything you want, piano lessons, horseback riding …*

I do not want to have anything to do with that goddamned Nazi, the sentence jolts her like a lightning strike, it gnaws at her stomach, she feels it climbing up into her throat, she jumps up and runs to the bathroom. There she stands, bent over the sink, puking, but she can't puke the sentence out of her, only the remnants of lunch. She turns on the faucet and holds her face in the cold stream of water.

And then Mrs. Fachinger comes in and takes care of her, helps her clean up, and leads her back.

The others have likely told Meta Levin who she is because the woman waves her over to her and says, "I'm so sorry, I didn't know," but her voice doesn't sound like she's really sorry. Johanna sits down and just waits for it all to be over, and when Mrs. Levin invites her to stop by for a visit the next morning if she wants to talk about it, she thinks, *I'm not going to do that, ever, it's happened and can't be changed.* But then she did end up going, she sat in the small living room and listened to what this woman needed to get off her chest. And she met Doron, her grandson, that arrogant medical student who spoke only English with her even though you could tell that he understood every word of German.

Suddenly a dog starts barking angrily as he rushes toward the fence she's running past, and she's startled, and strangely the barking calms her down, it brings her back to the present. She feels how wet her face is, from tears or rain, it's cold, a cold fall night, her shivers are from the rain and wind, it has nothing to do with air conditioning.

She folds her arms over her chest and pulls her hands inside the sleeves, but it doesn't warm her up. Her father's right, she really is full of herself, she's a snotty brat playing judge and jury—and along with her fury at her father there's also pity.

Mrs. Levin, she thinks. *What really happened back then, did you tell me only your version of the truth? What am I supposed to believe? My father doesn't lie, why would he tell me something that's not so? Could it be that you're fooling yourself, that you're dreaming about riches that were already gone by then? You often hear about people remembering their childhoods through rose-colored glasses, why should you be any different? You're an old woman, maybe you're just confusing everything. Here in town everyone, really everyone, says that my father is a decent man, when I saw Mrs. Tschernowski a couple of days ago she kept saying, "Your father is a decent man, Johanna." No one speaks badly of my father, Mrs. Levin. It's true I've never really gotten along with him that well, no, that's not true, I've never been that close to him, why, I don't know, either. "He doesn't talk much," my mother says, but he's not someone to be ashamed of, plenty of people are out there with fathers to be ashamed of. I've always been able to say, "My father is Robert Riemenschneider," and no one has ever made a face or a snide comment about him. My grandfather was a Nazi, Mrs. Levin, that's true, but didn't he actually do you a favor by buying the store from your family?*

She stands in front of Daniel's house, the shades to his window are drawn, there's light shining through the slit, the light in the bathroom is on, too, the living room is dark, you can see the flickering of the TV. She reaches out her hand to the doorbell, she longs to step into the warmth, imagining his mother giving her a towel to dry off her hair, and maybe she'll bring her a thick cardigan or a wool blanket to wrap herself up in and make her a cup of tea with rum or something else to warm her up. But then she pulls her hand back, she thinks she hears Daniel's voice, "Why did you run away?" he says. "Why did you give up so easily? Avoiding anything that's a bit too hard, that's a convenient strategy, isn't it?"

Johanna turns around, she trudges back up the street with heavy legs, fighting her way back through the rain, through puddles, she feels as if she'll drown if she doesn't find a safe place soon.

She's sopping wet when she pushes the garden gate open, the porch light over the door is on, a wide swath of light is shining onto the steps down to the street, the wet cobblestones glisten, the leaves of the rhododendron are casting narrow shadows that look like sharp, trembling spears. She has to force herself to step into the light, she stumbles up the steps, rummages around in her coat pocket until she finds the key, and opens the door.

Then she's standing in the entry hall, rain is running off her hair and coat, making a puddle on the floor, her shoes squeak as she moves.

Her mother comes out of the living room when she hears the front door, she's been waiting for her. She helps Johanna out of the coat and caresses her as though she were a little girl. "Should I make you some tea?" she says. "I'll run you a bath, you'll see. A nice hot bath works wonders, you'll be feeling better in no time."

Johanna is happy to let her mother fuss, after all she's "just a child who's full of herself," she doesn't want anything else to do with it, it has nothing to do with her, the whole story happened so long ago, there's no reason to let it drive her crazy.

When Johanna comes down to breakfast, she's relieved to see that her father has already left, she knows what kind of expression he would have been wearing at the table, what kind of tone he would have used to ask for the bread, just to make sure that she would sense his irritation. She stood up to him—he doesn't tolerate that. Her mother strokes her hair as she walks by and says, "He'll calm down again eventually, just show him that you didn't mean it that way," and Johanna thinks, *But maybe I did mean it that way.*

He's not around for dinner, either, that happens sometimes. Florian has already set the table, Johanna is amazed at how eager he is, he gets the bowl with the steaming potatoes from the kitchen, her mother brings in the goulash that Mrs. Maurer made, and the salad. "Dad can't make it to dinner," she says. "We'll have to eat alone," and Johanna wonders if he's staying away on purpose, then she thinks, *He doesn't take me that seriously,* and suppresses the anger that's rearing in her again.

They eat in silence, they all seem to be dwelling on their own thoughts. She absolutely has to work some more on her article about Hanna Bär, Mrs. Fachinger told her today, they have to turn in the articles in three days so that she can hand them off to the printer on time. Dominik and Kerstin aren't done yet, either, but both of them said they'd have no trouble making the deadline.

"And what about you, Johanna?" Mrs. Fachinger asked, and she just shrugged. "It doesn't absolutely have to be fifteen pages," Mrs. Fachinger said. "You've already turned in a good article about Palestine during the Mandate Period."

She meant it to be encouraging, but the hard part wasn't the number of pages, she's already finished twelve, but the fact that she was missing a personal element, something to add atmosphere and color to her article. If she'd picked Meta Levin, she would have compared her appearance and the circumstances of her life to those of Mrs. Neuberger. She might even have talked about the touch-ups she has imagined and gone into detail about the similarities and differences in their clothes and mannerisms, but Hanna Bär was so reticent and distant that Johanna can't think of anything, there's nothing at all. Melanie has offered to help her several times, but she keeps saying no. *Maybe I should take Melanie up on it after all,* she thinks now.

Florian suddenly sets his fork down onto his plate so hard that it startles them, he looks at their mother and says, a little too loud, "It starts at four, can't you drive me over there just this once, Mom?"

Mom draws her eyebrows together, it obviously takes a minute for her mother to get what he's talking about, and then she glances at her watch and says, "It's not even two yet, you can take the bus, Florian."

He pushes his plate away and says more quietly than before,

"That's not the point." And when he sees her expression, he lowers his face, pouting, and then it bursts out of him, "The other kids always have someone there to watch them when we play another team, their moms or sometimes even their dads, but not me, I never have anyone." He bites his lip, then wipes his napkin over his mouth, then his eyes, now he's speaking so quietly that they can hardly understand him, "Grandpa used to come sometimes, but he stopped last year, he wasn't interested anymore."

Mom holds out her hand, touches his arm, but he pulls it away and scoots his chair back, the feet of his chair squeak on the rug. "I can't," she says, depressed. "We've got two sales-rep appointments this afternoon, we've absolutely got to order a few more things for the Christmas season, I really just can't, Florian," and when she sees his disappointed face, she quickly adds, "Next time I'll try," and Johanna thinks that she must already be feeling guilty, and she doesn't know who she's more sorry for right now, Florian or Mom, the whole situation is just way too familiar.

"This time it's the sales reps," Florian says, "and the next time someone will be sick, or the tax adviser will be coming, or you'll be rearranging a department, or a new order will be in, or you'll have to get your hair done ..." His voice breaks, but he composes himself again quickly, his mouth with the nicely curved lips he inherited from his mother narrows when he says, "It's fine, it's not the end of the world."

He's only twelve, Johanna thinks, *and he's young for twelve, he's a kid,* and she remembers how sad she used to be that her parents so rarely had time, there was always some reason why they couldn't make it to a tournament or a school play, not even to career day, "Why should I go, Johanna? You're good in school, anyway, and

I've got so much to get done today, surely you understand." Of course she had understood, they were logical reasons, not excuses, but it didn't mitigate her disappointment, she knows how her brother is feeling right now, so she quickly says, "You know what, Flori? I'll drive you over."

She sees his face brighten, he jumps up so high his chair tips back against the wall. "Really?" he yells, hugging her, beaming, and says to his mother, "Johanna's coming with me, did you hear? Johanna's coming with me," as though she weren't there, but maybe he just wants to show her how happy he is.

Mom flashes Johanna a grateful look and says, "Can you afford to, isn't your English exam coming up?"

Johanna sees Florian tense up, his lips narrow again, which is why she says with emphatic nonchalance, "I'm good at English, nothing can go wrong, ever since that summer in England I've been unbeatable." And when she sees Florian relax again, she thinks, *And I'll still get the article on Hanna Bär done, too, it won't be that hard.*

"You can take the car," Mom says. "The key is on the bureau in the hallway, I'll call for a taxi to go to work in, and then Dad can drive me home." She stands up. "I've got to get going, good luck, Florian." She gives him a kiss, strokes Johanna's hair, and thanks her one more time.

Florian whistles loudly while he clears the table, and Johanna goes upstairs to put on something more comfortable.

On the way in the car, he tells her about their last few matches, about Mr. Berger, his gym teacher, who's also the team coach, and how many goals he's made this summer, more than the other boys. He describes every single one—who passed him the ball and how he caught it, "And I made one goal off a header, Johanna, I was wondering myself if I had it in me." She listens to him and thinks, ashamed, *I should have come and watched him before, he's my little brother and he'll be alone a lot once I'm in Israel.*

When they arrive at the stadium, the sun is breaking through the clouds. Florian looks up at the sky and says, "That's a good omen, we're going to win," and she thinks, *Why are you so sure that it's a good omen for your team, it could also be meant for the other team,* but she doesn't say it out loud, she's much too happy to see how excited he is.

They're all standing in front of the passage to the locker rooms, the players and their parents, and when Johanna and Florian get closer they can hear yelling and screaming, "Florian's here, hey Florian!" A tall, thin man in a blue tracksuit and glasses with bright red frames steps away from the group and approaches them. "My sister brought me!" Florian calls.

The man extends his hand, "Hi, I'm Mr. Berger," he says. "I'm Florian's gym teacher, it's nice you could come along, you can be really proud of your brother, he's our best striker."

Florian is beaming, he doesn't flinch when the man slaps him on the back the way the boys at her school slap each other on the back to say hello, even Daniel does it, although he also makes fun of it a lot, what he calls "affection among men."

Mr. Berger pushes Florian toward the locker room, "Get going, it's time," he calls loudly.

From behind in his jeans and parka, his blue duffel bag over his left shoulder, he looks so different to Johanna that it's hard for her to pick him out from the other boys wearing similar clothes as she watches them disappear into the little building. She looks quickly at the group of mothers, Melanie's mother is there, one of Melanie's brothers must be playing, too, but she doesn't know which one of the three, she doesn't think she'll recognize him, either.

Johanna looks for a seat in the stands, picking one right in the middle and far enough up that she has a good view of the entire field. When she arrived she was surprised at how many people there were, but now that the spectators are sitting down, the big stadium seems quite empty. The rows to the right and left in front of her are filled with excited, giggling, and whispering girls, probably schoolmates of the players. A lot of the girls are tall and well developed, others still look like children, and Johanna thinks of Nicole, the girl who used to be her friend who was always a whole head shorter than her. The other kids used to make fun of them, "Lookit, the giraffe and her flea," it never bothered her, they were friends. *Too bad she moved away,* Johanna thinks now, *and too bad we stopped writing letters.*

The girls jump to their feet and cheer as the boys run onto the field in blue and red jerseys. Johanna recognizes Florian, she sees his face searching the stands, and he waves at her when he finds her. She waves back, a couple of girls turn around curiously. *He's kind of a good-looking guy*, she thinks. *He'll have an easy time with the girls later on, and then people will stop asking if anyone asked him to dance, all he has to do is grow up, and it'll go smoothly for him.*

His legs are still tan from summer, you can see the light-colored scar on his thigh even from here. He had an accident last year when he was riding his bike to school, according to the police officer, he sped right through an intersection without looking both ways, right in front of a car that didn't have enough time to brake, the driver was not cited. Florian was in the hospital for two months, the compound fracture wasn't the worst part, it was the compound depressed skull fracture—they didn't know for a couple of days whether he would survive the accident. Johanna remembers the mood at home, the fear, and remembers him lying in the hospital bed, with tubes in his arm and nose, pale and strange and very, very small. Afterward their parents forbade him from riding his bike to school.

The referee blows his whistle, both teams take off running, Florian's team in blue, their opponents in red.

"Do you have a brother who's playing?" asks a boy as he sits down next to her, she looks to her side, he must be about as old as she is, and he's really good-looking, with blue eyes and light blond, almost white stubble, a strong, straight nose, and thick, curved eyebrows. But the nicest part is his eyes, big and set far apart. *Like a blond Doron,* she thinks, taken aback, turning her head and just nodding, and when he asks, "Which one is he?" she says curtly, "Number ten, in blue."

"A striker," he says knowingly. "Mine is the goalie for Gutenberg."

The ball goes back and forth, the boys run, both coaches stand on the sidelines spurring their teams on. Red and blue commingle, once in a while one of them falls down, then several plow into each other and the referee blows his whistle until they untangle themselves. Johanna has never been interested in soccer, she doesn't understand the rules, but she gets swept away by the thrill of it, and when the blue team gets a goal, she jumps up and yells just as enthusiastically as the girls sitting down to the left in front of her, and when there's a goal for red she hides her face in her hands and moans. Florian scores, she jumps up, screams, "Way to go, Florian!" and he turns around toward her, waving and laughing either at her or at the girls, she can't tell which.

The game continues, she's enjoying the thrill of the ball

moving back and forth. She gets hot sitting in the sun, she unbuttons her jacket, *the boys are lucking out with the weather.* She thinks of Uncle Hubert, who was never able to move like Florian, and she remembers how difficult it was for him to hobble up the path to the chalet from the parking lot on his two crutches. But they had had good luck with the weather that day, too, it had been warm and clear, and the views from the top were excellent. They didn't talk much during that excursion, Uncle Hubert was quiet and distracted, probably engrossed in thoughts and memories that he didn't want to share with her, but when she dropped him back off and said good-bye, he caressed her cheek with his trembling fingers and thanked her with tears in his eyes. *I should bring Florian out there some time*, she thinks, *he's just as much his great-uncle as mine, maybe it'd be good for Florian to see that there are men out there who are very different from Dad or these athletes here, and that lots of people have very different lives from those who've inherited money.*

She's missed something on the field, all the boys on the opposing team have suddenly formed a wall, their hands protecting their crotches the way she's seen on soccer games on TV, and she has to laugh, thinking, *They don't even have that much to protect yet.*

"A free kick," the blond Doron says beside her. A blue player passes the ball to Florian, who shoots the ball into the goal, the goalie makes a flying dive and lands in the wrong corner and is now rolling over toward where the ball went, and the boy next to Johanna sighs, "Wow, your brother faked him out pretty good, mine had no idea where he was aiming."

Johanna nods, and the solution to the problem with her article suddenly pops into her head. Hanna Bär's request that she should set a stone on her grandparents' grave could give her a way to compare the Jewish cemetery that Samuel and Ruth Wertheimer are buried in to the big cemetery in Jerusalem—where Hanna Bär probably won't be buried, she'll be buried in the cemetery on her kibbutz, but maybe some of the other Victoria alumnae will be.

First they took in the amazing view of the city from up on the Mount of Olives, it's the most beautiful view there is of Jerusalem, which she overheard a guide telling another group of tourists, in English with a heavy Israeli accent, "The most beautiful view of the Holy City." The hewn stones, white with an ocher glow, which all the buildings are made of were gleaming in the sun. Jerusalem, the city of gold, the city of copper and light, with its mosques, churches, and synagogues, with the golden cupola of the Dome of the Rock. Even from up there you could see the slope with the graves, here on the Mount of Olives is where the Prophets were buried, many Jews are buried here, too, who came here to Eretz Yisrael from every country in the world to die and be buried in the Holy Land, at a place located outside the city walls, as required by the purity laws, but close enough to both of the two walled-up arcs in the wall around the Old City, close enough to the Golden Gate that the Messiah would come through at the end of days.

Johanna sees the slope before her, the white marble slabs that mark the graves, shimmering in the harsh sunlight, from up here they look like an irregular mosaic, a strange mixture of the foreign and the familiar, she sees the weeds between the cracked stones, cacti with gigantic blossoms, wind-tousled trees with flat crowns, palm trees.

They walked down the Mount of Olives in between the graves, reading inscriptions, counting the stones on top of the graves, they were enchanted by this place overhung by a strange, tense quiet where you had the feeling—even more so than in the city itself—of living somewhere outside of time—or rather, somehow in between two ages. Off in the distance they could hear the cry of a muezzin, then they heard bells chiming, the sounds floating through the air and dissolving, almost without anyone noticing them. "Many famous people are buried here," Mrs. Fachinger had said, leading them to the grave of Else Lasker-Schüler, a famous avant-garde poet and artist from Berlin.

If there's enough space, she thinks, *then I can also write about cemetery desecrations, I can talk about how the Arabs devastated the cemetery in 1948 and took out the headstones to use for building materials, and I could mention that people keep finding old Jewish headstones in building walls here in Germany, too, when they renovate buildings.*

Florian's team wins seven to four, the boys in the blue jerseys throw up their hands, the girls down to the left in front of her scream and wave, even the others down on the right are waving madly. The blond Doron next to Johanna stands up, "Oh well," he says, disappointed. "What can you do? Maybe it'll go different for the return match, will you be here for that game, too?"

She shrugs, "Maybe," she smiles. *He really does look good, and he can't help it that he looks so much like Doron.* She nods good-bye to him and heads down to the field. They're standing in front of the passage to the locker rooms, Florian looks so different from how he does at home, he's beaming, his friends are crowding around him patting him on the shoulder, a couple of girls are waiting for him off to the side.

"Johanna!" Florian calls, running to her, he's crazed with excitement, "I made three goals, did you see, it's so cool you could come today, I'm not always that good ..."

She laughs and hugs him, and suddenly she recognizes the

little boy he used to be. How happy he was before he started going to school, she remembers how she made his goodie bag, a tradition for little kids on their first day of school, really a huge cone made of cardboard that Johanna had decorated with colorful papers and ribbons, and then she and her mother filled it with all his favorite candy, and she had even spent her own allowance to buy him a stuffed pink pig for good luck in school, but it didn't help that much.

After a bit, Florian invites her to the post-game celebration at the ice-cream parlor. They drive into the Old City, to Daniel's and her favorite café. How often they had sat here on the patio over the summer, they always used to meet here when they were just starting to date but didn't dare to go over to each other's houses yet, when they still didn't know what would become of this fledgling romance or whether anything would come of it at all, although she later said she knew right after the summer carnival at school that they would sleep with each other at some point, and Daniel said he had hoped so, too, but he didn't know it yet, *girls really do seem to know these things first.*

Florian orders a chocolate sundae with whipped cream, and she orders a coffee float. They're sitting at a table by the window, you can see the river from here, the tree-covered slope up to the hunting chalet. A flock of birds in the sky soars past. *This might be my last chance for ice cream this year,* Johanna thinks, looking out at the patio, the umbrellas have been folded up and the chairs are leaning against the tables, soon they'll be cleared away until next spring. Now a couple of sparrows are hopping around among yellow leaves that the wind is blowing over the flagstones. Winter hasn't come yet, but especially at night you can feel it already.

"Why did you and Dad have that fight yesterday?" Florian

suddenly asks, and she says, "Do you remember that time we drove down to the Adriatic with the tent?" He shakes his head, she counts back, the last time he couldn't have been more than five, no wonder he doesn't remember.

"Well, Dad used to be different then," she says, and she tells him about the father who used to build sand castles with her, who used to romp around in the waves, and who would run after the ice-cream man with them. *He really did use to be pretty different,* she thinks, *away from home, away from the store, maybe away from his father,* and she wonders whether it's a relief for him that his father's dead, but of course that's not something you're allowed to think, much less say out loud.

"Was Grandpa really a Nazi?" Florian asks, and she nods.

"But it was Hitler who murdered the Jews," Florian says, and she says, "So, what, you think he single-handedly strangled every single one of the six million? Do you know how many that is, six million? That's five times the size of Munich, almost ten times the size of Frankfurt, or twice the size of Berlin, you know how big Berlin has gotten, imagine that number of people. Do you really think Hitler killed them all personally?"

Florian is confused, "But what did Grandpa have to do with it?" he asks.

"I'd like to know myself," she says, and when she sees his frightened face she feels sorry, she knows how it feels when a shadow is suddenly cast over love and you don't know anymore what's under the shadow, whether anything is left at all.

"He didn't kill any Jews," she says, "I'm pretty certain of that."

"What'd he do, then?" he asks, "Why did you guys get so mad yesterday and why did you scream at each other like that, you and Dad?"

"I don't know," she says, "I don't know what Grandpa did," without answering his question about the reason for the fight. "I don't know, but when I find out I'll tell you. I promise that I'll talk to you about it. Anyway, come on, we've got to get back home, otherwise they'll start worrying and maybe start thinking you lost when you actually won!"

It works, that's distracted him, he laughs, he claps his hands once and yells, "Oh man, did we ever, seven to four! And I made three goals!"

The mood at dinner is tense, and it doesn't help when Mom asks about the soccer game and Florian starts to tell her about it, at first with a certain amount of joy, but then his voice grows softer and softer and he pauses in between words, as though he doesn't know how to continue, and finally he just clams up.

Johanna looks over at her father, their eyes meet. *He doesn't look angry,* she thinks, *at least not like he's going to scream at me again.* He's searching her face, she pouts her lips a little, lowers her face, holding it a bit crooked and thinks, *Now I look the way I do in that old picture from when I was a kid that he has on his desk.* She doesn't know if she knew back when that picture was taken the power that that face exerts on him, but now she knows. It's one of the weapons in her repertoire, even if she's a little ashamed of using it.

For a moment it's just the two of them at the table, and then she asks him if he could use her help on Saturday. "I haven't been to the store in a long time," she says. "I'd like to come help."

He lowers his eyes, the corners of his mouth twitch, and he says, "Yes, of course, there are a lot of people out with the flu, Mrs. Müller-Meinert would be delighted if you could come in, she asks about you all the time."

"Maybe you can also take a look at the Christmas decorations the window dressers are planning for this year," her mother says. "Florian, pass me your plate."

Well, that wasn't so hard now, was it, Johanna thinks, standing up to help her mother clear the table.

The words *Riemenschneider's Fine Apparel, Coats & Leather* are large and curved, the bright red letters match the soft, rosy beige shade of the hewn sandstone, it looks elegant, but not showy. *Actually a historical marker should be put up on this building, too, like there is on the back wall of the parking lot where the old synagogue used to be, a historical marker that reads: This is the former site of the women's apparel shop Heimann & Compagnie, founded in 1896 by Moritz Heimann, the grandfather of Meta Heimann, whose name is now Meta Levin and who resides in Jerusalem, which was acquired in 1938 by the grandfather of Johanna Katharina Riemenschneider under somewhat vague circumstances.*

The building looks different from the old pictures that Johanna has seen in the city archives, someone must have installed the big display windows at some point when people weren't as concerned about historical preservation because, when her grandfather had wanted to do a big renovation in the sixties, the Office for Historical Preservation had required him to retain the façade and renovate only the interior spaces. She recalls that he had wanted to enlarge the windows on the second and third stories at the time, too, but she's glad that they rejected that plan. The façade with its hewn sandstone is simply beautiful. After the last cleaning a couple of years ago, the color of the stone is now light and bright, only in the cracks and crevices has it begun to darken again already. *How did the building look back when you were a kid, Mrs. Levin?*

Johanna walks up to the wide glass door that opens in front of her automatically, a warm flood of air hits her. She nods, smiles, returns the hellos of the salespeople, heads past the Young Fashion department that her parents set up just four or five years ago, and takes the escalator up to the second floor to Women's. On the way, she pulls her name tag out of her coat pocket, she's had it since she was fifteen and started helping out in the store sometimes on Saturdays and during shorter school vacations.

Her father is always pointing out that it's a way for her to make some extra money, but that's not why she does it, she knows that. Riemenschneider's is a family company, he wants his children to be a part of the store, especially her, the eldest, in case Florian doesn't want to or can't. Florian's not at all dumb, but he has a hard time concentrating, and so far, except for sports, he hasn't shown any particular inclination toward anything, and certainly not for clothes. He really doesn't care how the clothes he wears look so long as the brand name is right.

She isn't that interested in clothes, either. At least, she's way less interested than the other girls her age, and she hasn't worn anything from Riemenschneider's for years, she buys her clothes in other stores, clothes that are exceedingly simple, exceedingly cheap. "Oh, Johanna, it's just not appropriate for you to dress so shabbily!" Mom always used to complain at first. "What will people think? Your parents run a clothing store and you're running around like the daughter of God knows who. It's not appropriate, you should always be dressed impeccably."

Dad of all people had defended her. "Oh, let her be," he had said. "That's just her way of dealing with having so many things available to her. I mean, I'd like her to dress differently, too, but I can understand where she's coming from. I used to have to wear trousers with freshly pressed creases in them every day while all the other boys were wearing jeans. So I won't force her to dress the way I'd like her to, as far as I'm concerned she should go right on playing things down if she wants."

"Good morning, Johanna!" says Mrs. Müller-Meinert. "It's so nice to have you here helping out again! It's only the middle of October, but business has been like December—it feels like the Christmas sales start earlier and earlier every year."

Her whole, wide face lights up with laughter, and Johanna laughs, too. She really likes this woman. She's known her for as long as she can remember. Before, when she was still little, she'd called her Auntie Müller, and she used to come over anytime she was sick and her mother had to go to the store. *Demoted to baby-sitting*, Johanna thinks now. Auntie Müller used to read out loud to her and sing with her. In fact, all the children's songs she knows, she learned from her, her mother can't sing, "unfortunately," as she always laments.

"Oh, Auntie Müller," Johanna slips, remembering how sad it was when she had to stop calling her Auntie and switch to Mrs., but her parents thought it was appropriate that way. The laughing disappears from Mrs. Müller-Meinert's face and turns into a small, nostalgic smile. "Oh, Johanna, we've both grown older." And then, businesslike again, she adds, "Maybe you'd better put on something from the store, it's better that way, it doesn't make such a good impression if you're wearing something from another store." And when Johanna nods, the woman walks over to one of the display cubbies and pulls out a simple red sweater and holds it out to her. "Here, this one will definitely look good on you."

Johanna changes in one of the dressing rooms, she puts on her name tag, stows her coat and T-shirt under the counter, and then she gets to work. The blouses and skirts on the racks have to be hung neatly, sorted by size, before the customers start coming and mixing them up again. It's early right now, there are only a few women in the store, three or four dressing rooms are occupied.

Then Johanna straightens up the T-shirts. She's done this so often she doesn't need a table to fold them on anymore, she can do it in midair. Pick it up, shake it out, fold back the sleeves, each one along with a narrow strip of the front of the shirt, then fold it in half in the middle, one fold it's a short T-shirt, two folds if it's a long one, she doesn't particularly need to concentrate, her hands do the work on their own. *Did you ever actually help out in the store, Mrs. Levin? What did it used to look like, was it still like the pictures from 1910 that I saw in the city archives? This area here on the second floor didn't used to be retail space, this is where the workshops were for the dressmakers and furriers and milliners, and the third floor was where the proprietors lived, your grandparents. When you were little, did you live here, too, or in the house on Tuchwebergasse, the cloth weavers' street, that my grandfather bought along with the store, where my father was later born?*

The store itself used to be on the ground floor, and it looked quite different. It was divided into rooms, and in each room there were long, high counters that the employees stood behind, men in narrow suits with high collars, or women with luxurious, pinned-up hair and tightly laced corsets, and they took the things that the customers wanted to see down from the shelves, spreading them out on the tables for customers who were also wearing long skirts and tight corsets. Even the mannequins in the tall, narrow display windows looked that way. You never saw any women like that, either, Mrs. Levin. When you were a child, women didn't wear laced corsets anymore. Were all the rooms still intact when you were here, like in those old pictures, or had all the walls already been ripped out?

There weren't escalators yet, in any case. Just these wide, curved stairways in the middle. I was still little, maybe five or six, when the escalators were put in, I can still remember begging my grandfather to take me on the escalator, up and down, up again, down again, it was thrilling. You'd be amazed, Mrs. Levin, if you saw the building now. Well, you probably did see it when the mayor hosted that event for you, even if you didn't go inside and meet my grandfather, that goddamned Nazi.

The store slowly fills up, Johanna helps customers, she brings clothes into the dressing rooms, asks if they fit "or would you like me to bring another size?" And then she takes the clothes away again once they've been tried on and are no longer needed.

Suddenly Mrs. Neuberger is standing in front of her. "Ah, Ms. Riemenschneider, you're helping your parents today, that's so nice."

She really does look a lot like Mrs. Levin, Johanna thinks, but suddenly she realizes that she's actually no longer sure what Mrs. Levin looks like, the touched-up face Johanna's created for herself has displaced the original, like two negatives set on top of each other, and Mrs. Neuberger and Mrs. Levin now look like twins. "Can I help you with anything?" she asks, confused, and Mrs. Neuberger says, "I'm looking for a sweater, something pretty and warm …"

Johanna spreads out sweaters for her, one after the other, although she soon knows which piece Mrs. Neuberger is going to pick, but the woman takes her time, clearly enjoying trying things on. Johanna suppresses a smile as she takes the absurdly expensive cashmere sweater set over to the register—she guessed right. *It really looks fabulous on her, too, she's petite enough to wear something like it, and the dusty rose is flattering with her gray hair. This'd look good on you, too, Mrs. Levin, but in Israel it doesn't get that cold, so you don't need any cashmere, although everyone says that some years it snows in Jerusalem. Of course, the snow apparently doesn't stay on the ground long, but for one or two hours the city of gold is white, they say. I have a hard time believing that, it was the end of April when we were there, and it was awfully hot. For me, Israel is a land of warmth, of longing, and I can't imagine a more beautiful city than Jerusalem.*

Even poverty is picturesque in Jerusalem, she thinks, and immediately she reprimands herself. *Don't be so arrogant, you have no idea what poverty means, you get a nice allowance, more than most kids your age, your parents aren't stingy, never were. You've never had to think about whether you can afford to go to the movies or get ice cream, you can buy any book that you'd like, any CD, and when you want something, you get it. And now on top of that you've inherited a pile of money, so much that you have no idea what you could possibly spend it on, you're really the last person who should be saying anything about the esthetics of poverty.*

She remembers how she had fasted a few years ago just to experience what hunger actually feels like, which she had known only from books. She had eaten only stale bread and water. For four days she kept it up, then she started getting light-headed and felt so weak that she had to start eating again. She had been really proud of herself, but at the same time it was clear to her that the whole thing was just a show, a farce, because obviously she could have gone to the fridge at any time and eaten her fill, whereas people who are truly poor often don't even have stale bread, maybe nothing but water.

"Johanna, do you think you could go down to Young Fashion?" Mrs. Müller-Meinert says. "They just called up, they've got a rush down there and wondered if we could send someone down."

Johanna nods and takes the escalator down to the ground floor. She doesn't like working in Young Fashion because sometimes people she knows from school come in. It's embarrassing for her to wait on them, and even more embarrassing if someone says "that's too expensive" or "I can't afford that," and she feels the envy behind it, the unspoken: *You've got it good, you can have anything you want.* She's glad when the manager sends her to the jeans section, not only because she knows jeans and almost never guesses the wrong size, but also because jeans are more innocuous than tops, the price differences aren't as big.

There didn't use to be a Young Fashion department, Mrs. Levin. If you want, I'll take some pictures for you of the different departments and I'll bring them to you when I come to Israel next year. Yes, I'm coming, right after graduation, I'll put off college for a year and work in Israel, not on a kibbutz, I don't seem to have inherited my family's farming genes, I think I'll work in a nursing home. I've also started learning Hebrew, secretly, because I haven't told my parents about my plan yet, I'm afraid of the fight we're going to have. I can just hear my father saying, "You should major in business, something that will benefit the store, why do you want to go to a foreign country you have no relationship to?" How can I explain to him that I really do have a relationship to it, something I'm looking for in this foreign country. Maybe you're it, Mrs. Levin, please stay alive, I still need you.

"Hi, Johanna," someone says suddenly from behind her just as she's grabbing a couple of pairs of jeans from a dressing room to tidy it up. It's Kerstin. "I need some new pants, a black pair, do you have something nice?"

Johanna winces at the sound of her voice, she forces herself to smile as she goes over to the racks with Kerstin, but Kerstin doesn't notice Johanna's discomfort, she's talking about a party that she's going to with her boyfriend, and she needs something new to wear. And then when she comes out of the changing room with her zipper still open so that you can see her tanned stomach and pierced belly button, she says, "Oh, I've finished my article for Mrs. Fachinger, finally. I picked Fanny Goldmann, and she's so much more boring than the woman you picked, Hanna Bär, you picked her right before I was going to. Fanny Goldmann spent the whole time talking about her grandkids, otherwise nothing, she's just a housewife and mother and grandmother." Kerstin snickers. "Do you know what I did? I wrote about what she cooks for her grandkids, what they like to eat. And I described what an Israeli breakfast looks like, with cucumbers, tomatoes, and bell peppers with herring and lakerda instead of cold cuts like we have in Germany, because you can't eat meat and milk together—otherwise it's not kosher. I also wrote about the dietary laws. And then I added a recipe for gefilte fish, do you remember her talking about how she also used to have gefilte fish in Germany every Friday evening for Shabbat and that her children and grandchildren always ask for it?"

"Where did you get the recipe?" Johanna asks and thinks, *That was a good idea for her article, I hadn't thought Kerstin was so creative.*

"I bought an Israeli cookbook," Kerstin says. "Everything's in it. What do you think, should we make an Israeli meal for the school history group maybe, with hummus as an appetizer? We can get canned chickpeas at the Turkish grocery, you just have to purée it, I tried it out, and they've got tahini, too, in Turkish it's called *tahin*, it's sesame seeds but ground a bit more coarsely than they do in Israel, and if you mix in enough garlic and lemon juice, it tastes really good."

"That's a great idea," Johanna says, and she means it sincerely. "So when?"

"How about two weeks from today?" Kerstin says. "I can't next Saturday. Everyone could meet in the afternoon on the Saturday afterward, and then everyone would still have the evening free."

Johanna nods, "Sure, that sounds great," and suddenly she feels satisfied, almost joyful, and it'll even be fun working with Kerstin to come up with the menu.

As she leaves the store around two o'clock, a little tired and hungry, she pauses in the middle of Marktplatz, turns around and contemplates this building that has played such an important role for her family and that she was always so proud of, a feeling that is now conflicted at the very least. She looks up at the third floor where Mrs. Levin's grandparents had lived, surely she spent a lot of time with them there, because her parents must also have spent the majority of their time there, like Johanna's. She tries to picture Mrs. Levin as a child, as a teenager, but she can't, she can only picture Mrs. Neuberger, the way she probably looked when she was a child, a thin, small girl with a coronet braid around the top of her head.

I'm writing about Hanna Bär, Mrs. Levin, not about you, I didn't feel confident enough to pick you, not just because of my parents but also because of my classmates and the gossip it would have created. I guess I really should have picked you, but actually I'm happy now that I picked Hanna Bär. I read Melanie's article, she describes you accurately and sympathetically, but she only just touched on the issue with the store. Moritz was right: Melanie's report is a little boring, but I'm grateful for it.

Suddenly it occurs to her that she forgot to stop by the publicity department and take a look at the Christmas decorations they're planning, but she doesn't care, it'll be the usual St. Nicholases and angels, the stylized snowflakes, and if they're up for a change of pace for once they'll put up some reindeer. She smiles, turns back around, and heads over to the bus stop, her father's staying at work, so she has to take the bus home.

Did you catch that just now, Mrs. Levin? Even Kerstin was impressed by Israel. I'm excited to hear what you'll say when you finally get to see the annual, you and the other women. A tribute to the living, the way the stones at the cemetery are a memorial to the dead. By the way, I also set a stone on the graves of Moritz Heimann and his wife, Rosa, an especially reddish pebble from you, and a small white one from Doron.

The bus is full, Johanna is standing on the platform, boxed in between strange bodies, her nose filled with strange smells, her ears penetrated by strange voices. She's sorry she didn't wait for her father, she could have gone to a café for a while and done some reading, or she could at least have walked to the train station and caught a bus there, the bus is always less crowded from there. The pressure from the strange bodies is unpleasant for her, the air is so stuffy that she tries to take only shallow breaths, and the strange hairs that brush across her cheeks and lips as a woman pushes past her give her goose bumps. *Maybe I should talk to Dad again,* she thinks, *to see if he would agree to my buying a car now and not waiting until after graduation. I mean, it's not like I can't afford it.*

When the bus stops in front of the train station, so many passengers get off that Johanna breathes a sigh of relief and sinks into one of the seats that has just freed up. She presses close to the window and looks out, thinking, *I could've used something to eat, too, some pizza, maybe, there won't be anything at home.*

"No family lunch today," Mom had announced at breakfast. "Everybody can make themselves a sandwich, I just don't have time today, I've got to get dinner ready for company tonight."

"Who's coming over?" Johanna asked, and Mom answered, "Lutz Bauer and his wife, the Hermanns from next door, and Mr. Mayer from the bank and his wife." And when Johanna made a face, she quickly added, "Just a small, casual get-together," but Johanna knew Mom would spend the whole afternoon in the kitchen with Mrs. Maurer preparing all the different little hors d'oeuvres to eat.

The bus slows, stops, the woman sitting across from her stands up, gathers her overstuffed cloth shopping bag and two bulging plastic ones that had been sitting between her feet, and gets off. A young man in jeans and tennis shoes plops down into the open seat, pulls a paperback out of his jacket, and starts reading. Johanna looks down at his feet, which look small for a man, even in tennis shoes.

She doesn't look up, she doesn't want to see his face, she isn't at all curious what he's reading, she just stares at his tennis shoes, remembering that she had once sat on a bus and looked at tennis shoes like these and also thought, *His feet are very small for a man.* That was in Jerusalem, with Doron, on the way to his dorm. As this memory comes over her, she can picture his feet in his slightly dirty tennis shoes, then his bare feet, tan, hardly larger than Florian's, only bonier and with longer toes, and on the rag rug in his dorm room after he took off his shoes and socks, standing—he didn't sit down on his bed—she suddenly feels the excitement again, that mixture of fear and lust, which wasn't really lust, more a thirst for adventure, and curiosity. She can't take her eyes off the young man's shoes and is relieved when the bus stops and she has to get off.

The kitchen smells like frying liver, thyme, onions, garlic, her mother is making one of her amazing pâtés as an hors d'oeuvre.

“How’d it go today?” she asks, and Johanna shrugs and says, “How else, tiring.”

Her mother smiles at her briefly and says, “I put something out for you on the dining table,” and when Johanna looks at her inquisitively she says, “A worker’s got to eat!” Johanna flinches, that was a saying of her grandfather’s. She always used to ask him, “And what if someone can’t work?” and then he’d shrug, frown slightly, and say, “Anyone who wants to work can find a way.”

She imagines him and thinks, *Strange that it never occurred to me before how self-righteous and arrogant he was.* “I’m going to go lie down for a while after I eat,” she tells her mother, who nods and Johanna thinks, *A worker’s got to sleep, too.*

In her room she pulls the shades closed before she lies down on her bed in her clothes, she’s taken only her jacket and shoes off. But she can’t fall asleep, the memories won’t leave her alone, memories of Doron and thoughts of Daniel. For a long time she thought it wasn’t any of Daniel’s business what happened in Jerusalem, but secretly she always knew that she has no choice, she’s got to tell him, not just how everything started, which actually will be pretty easy for her to talk about. *On the day after we met the women in the Ticho House, I did end up going over to Mrs. Levin’s,* she’ll say, *although I actually didn’t want to. I called Mrs. Levin right after breakfast, then I let Mrs. Fachinger know, got into a taxi, and went over to her apartment at the seniors’ home in Mishkenot Sha’ananim, Meta Levin had written the address on a scrap of paper the night before, and on the way I asked the taxi driver to stop at a flower stand, and I bought seven white roses.*

The apartment was a small one with a kitchenette. Johanna offered Mrs. Levin the flowers and watched her find a suitable vase to put them in, then she followed her into the living room.

She was surprised to see a young man sitting there on the couch nodding hello to her. He muttered awkwardly, "Sorry, I didn't know you were having company, I don't want to interrupt …" But Mrs. Levin waved her hand dismissively, "You're not interrupting, this is Doron, my grandson, he visits me a lot, he's in medical school in Jerusalem." She set the vase with the roses on top of a glass cabinet made of light wood, behind a few randomly positioned family photos, offered Johanna the armchair, and sat down next to her grandson on the couch. There were three glasses on the glass coffee table with a carafe of orange juice next to a vase of blue chicory flowers.

The apartment was furnished simply, almost meagerly, but displayed a decided sense of elegance that Johanna had already noticed in Mrs. Levin during her interview, an elegance that did not depend on money, you could see it in her carefully chosen clothes, her measured movements, and her reserved speech. This was exactly why the phrase "that goddamned Nazi" had come across as so harsh, so striking.

She was a woman who obviously valued a refined environment, Johanna noticed immediately. The same care went into her choice of a yellow vase for the dried blue chicory flowers, the blue rug that she was standing on was a perfect match for the blue and yellow pattern of the throw on the couch. Even the family photos on the glass cabinet—arranged in an apparently random way—actually followed the principle by which the collector's teacups and saucers were organized behind the glass door, three, two, one, two, three, Johanna recognized the system as she kept avoiding eye contact with Mrs. Levin.

The woman was sitting on the couch, upright, without slouching, outwardly composed but inwardly excited, you could tell from the way she occasionally touched her grandson's hand. Johanna had never found out whether he had coincidentally come for a visit or whether she had asked him to come over for support, and she hadn't tried to find out, either. Doron was a good-looking young man in his early twenties who refused to say a single word in German although she could tell that he understood everything. He insisted on speaking English with Johanna, good English but with a harsh, crisp Israeli accent, and he spoke Hebrew to his grandmother, who he called *Safta*.

During the visit that morning, Mrs. Levin again talked about her sheltered, happy childhood and about the violin, she was fixated on the violin, and Johanna thinks that unfulfilled childhood dreams often nag at people their whole lives, maybe the grief over the things a person has lost actually grows stronger every year, no reality can ever truly put those kinds of dreams back into perspective.

And then Mrs. Levin brought up the store, "He stole it from us," she said. "Just stole it, and we didn't get anything for it, I don't know if my grandparents got any money, but my parents and I didn't, in any case."

"What happened to your grandparents?" Johanna asked.

Mrs. Levin raised her face and looked at her so directly that Johanna looked away. "You don't know?" she asked. "They committed suicide together after we fled, we found out about it from neighbors, they took poison, both of them, you can find their graves in the Jewish cemetery, Moritz and Rosa Heimann, passed away on January 18, 1940. 'Passed Away' is what the headstone says, but really it should read 'Murdered on January 18, 1940.' They were too old to flee, they didn't see any other way out."

Mrs. Levin started to weep, and Doron slid closer to her and put his arm around her, saying something in a deeply loving voice. *He really loves her,* Johanna thought, imagining her grandfather, remembering how it warmed her heart to caress his smooth head.

She didn't dare say anything else, she just answered the questions that Mrs. Levin had, about Johanna's parents, if they sometimes talk about the old times, if her grandfather ever talked about the origins of the store. She shook her head, "No, he never did, his stories always started after the war, during the famine years when he built the business back up selling clothes that local women working out of their homes could sew." *We didn't have a lot in those days, you can be happy that you were born only later, long after the hard times.* But she didn't say that out loud, it was clear to her that those kinds of worries couldn't be compared to what Mrs. Levin had experienced.

She didn't speak for most of the time, and Mrs. Levin grew quieter and quieter as well until the quiet hung heavily, becoming more and more unbearable between them. Johanna was relieved when Mrs. Levin stood up and said she had to go down to the dining hall now, for lunch, and held out her hand to Johanna, a thin, delicate hand with long, slender fingers, a hand made to play the violin, and Johanna thought of bending down to kiss it.

Doron stood up as well. They both accompanied Mrs. Levin down to the door of the dining hall, then they left the building. To Johanna's surprise, Doron said, "Come on, I can still show you a bit of the city as long as you're here."

He took her to the windmill that she had seen on the edge of town, told her about Sir Moses Montefiore, who had founded the first Jewish settlement in modern times here in Jerusalem, outside the city walls, back in the nineteenth century. "The windmill was intended as a place for the Jewish immigrants to work," he said, "but it wasn't ever actually put into business." And then he started to tell her about the time before the foundation of Israel, about the British Mandate government's anti-Jewish policies during the Nazi period in Germany. By keeping Jews from immigrating, the British also prevented many people in danger from being saved. In his raw English he said that, even after the end of World War II, when the whole world knew that six million Jews had been murdered, they refused to allow the desperate survivors to immigrate. It was no wonder that the Jews rose up and started fighting for their own country by force of arms, because ultimately they had experienced firsthand the destiny that would be in store for them as a minority in other countries, to be repeated again and again.

Johanna listened to him talk about arrests, house searches, and military operations, he spoke with such enthusiasm, how a right-wing underground Jewish organization called the Irgun blew up part of the King David Hotel in 1946, which was the headquarters of the British civil and military administration for the Mandate government.

Why is he telling me all this? she thought. *I don't want to hear anything about war and military operations, I'm interested in completely different things, like what life was like for people at that time, where did they come from, how did they manage to make the desert fertile, why are men always fascinated by acts of violence like this?* And fleetingly she remembered the glimmer of excitement in the eyes of her grandfather and his friend Friedrich Stamm when they would talk about their experiences during the war.

And then he suddenly asked, "Do you maybe want to see an Israeli university dormitory? We could go over to my place and have a cup of coffee, I make an excellent Arabic coffee with *hel*."

In retrospect, now, here, lying in her own bed, Johanna wonders why she was so willing to say yes, she doesn't know anymore why she just nodded, after a short hesitation that he probably didn't even notice. And she thinks, *Maybe I only wanted to show him that not all Germans are anti-Semitic, maybe I wanted to show him that it was a perfectly natural thing, which isn't how I actually felt, and I bet he didn't, either. My ancestors murdered his ancestors, and here we're drinking Arabic coffee with* hel *together. As though it were that simple.*

At the time, in front of the windmill, she pushed the thought of her grandfather, the goddamned Nazi, aside, as well as her memory of Mrs. Levin saying "He stole the store from us," she just nodded and walked over to the bus stop beside this unfamiliar young man. She was aware of how good-looking he was, she didn't need the glances of the other girls, curious and a little envious, to know that, but she noticed them and it was fun for her. She felt as if she was doing something bold, experiencing an adventure, abandoning herself to the sun, the heat, the beauty. She was filled with the color of the light stones, everywhere these huge, hewn stones in yellow-ocher shades, Jerusalem, the city of gold, of copper and light.

On the bus he stopped talking, he just stared out of the window, and his sudden silence stood like a wall between them. Johanna lowered her eyes, his feet were surprisingly small, even in the tennis shoes he had on, although it was so hot out, they looked quite dainty for a man. Doron was tall, at least half a head taller than her, but slim, jeans size 32 at most, closer to 31 probably, 36 inseam, she had to make an effort to keep pace with him.

The dorm was a gigantic apartment building that looked neither old nor new, just boring. Johanna was walking behind

Doron, he wasn't paying attention to her anymore, he just rushed on in silence, she almost had to run to keep up, and she had to fight the urge to just stop and watch him until he disappeared. Even in the elevator he didn't look at her, and she asked herself why he invited her at all, and she also asked herself why she said yes, she wasn't in the mood for coffee, and if she had been, she'd have preferred to sit out at one of the sidewalk cafés.

The elevator stopped, she followed him through a long corridor with a lot of doors, and her uneasiness grew stronger. The corridor was dim, the only light was coming through a window farther ahead. He stopped in front of one door, pulled a key out of his jeans pocket, and opened it. "Here we are," he said, and made an inviting hand motion, but then went into the room before her.

There were two beds in the room, one on the right wall and one on the left, in between were two tables shoved together and a couple of chairs. A boy was lying on the bed on the left, about as old as Doron, reading. When they came in, he put his book down, stood up, and said *shalom*. "This is Johanna," Doron said in English, and then he added a couple of sentences in Hebrew. The boy, a very dark, nice-looking guy, hardly taller than her, nodded at her, then he took a backpack, stuck his book inside, nodded at her one more time, smiled, and left the room without a word.

Johanna sat down at the table while Doron went to the back corner where there was a kitchen cabinet by a sink. She watched him tip a couple of teaspoons of coffee into a *finjan*, add sugar and some spice, and then pour water over it, lit a propane camping stove, and put the *finjan* onto the burner. Above the cabinet on the wall hung a poster, of Arafat and Peres and Rabin, who had jointly received the Nobel Peace Prize the previous year. On the wall between Doron's bed and a narrow bookcase hung a homemade paper skeleton. She suppressed a smile, she had had one just like it when she was younger, now it was in Florian's room.

The coffee hissed out, it gave off a strange, tangy smell, and she asked herself again why she had come along. She remembered Tanja and Birgit talking in the bathroom before the trip to Israel, she had come in and couldn't help overhearing everything they were saying. "Israeli men are totally hot," Tanja had said. "You can see in all the pictures, they've got really nice-looking guys there," and Birgit had said, "They're circumcised, do you know what that looks like?" Tanja had laughed. "I've got a cousin who was born with something called phimosis, and he had to have surgery when he was little, I bet it looks kind of like that." "Um, how do you know what your cousin's dick looks like?" Birgit asked. "Have you done anything with him?" Tanja scoffed, "You're crazy! I *meant,* I've seen him, when we were little kids, when we used to go swimming together, that's all."

Johanna was standing at the sink washing her hands. *Have you guys forgotten everything we learned in the orientation meetings?* she had thought. *About the history of the Jews, the founding of the State of Israel, have you just got boys on the brain, nothing but flirting, escapades?*

And now I'm the one sitting here in the room of an Israeli medical student, she thought, *and Tanja, Birgit, and the others are taking in some site or other without me.*

She stood up, went to the window, and looked down into the courtyard with its eucalyptus trees. "Mrs. Rappaport always thinks of the German woods," she says out loud, "and your *safta* always thinks of her violin." She turned around and asked, "Have you ever been to Germany?" He raised his face and angrily said, "No, I'll never set foot in that country where so many Jews were murdered." He gave her a look, "I'm wondering where you get the nerve to come to Israel at all." It wasn't a question, he doesn't give her any time to answer, either, he pours coffee into small cups and offers her one. "Here," he said.

The coffee tasted hot and sweet, really different from the coffee that she was familiar with, *hel* must be some kind of spice, like cinnamon or cardamom, she felt the coffee running down her throat, warming her from the inside, a strange feeling, stronger than from alcohol, which she didn't like, but then she wasn't sure anymore if this warm feeling was coming from the coffee or from him, because he took her cup out of her hand, set it on the table, and put his arm around her, with a harsh, assertive motion, devoid of any tenderness. Silently he unbuttoned her blouse, her pants, he peeled her clothes off her body and pressed her down onto his bed before he took off his T-shirt, tennis shoes, jeans, and underwear. She stole a glance at his erection, curious despite the fear that suddenly gripped her, a fear arising not from his nakedness, he was good-looking, with a delicate beauty that she liked, there was nothing threatening about his body, but nonetheless she felt threatened at that moment, it was something else that she couldn't explain. She wanted to say something, she wanted to ask for time, for a little tenderness, she wasn't ready yet, but he held her mouth closed, he threw himself over her with a determined look on his face and penetrated her without waiting for her to feel ready, it hurt, but she didn't say so, *caress me first, please,* she submitted to it, and she submitted to her own desire as it slowly awakened, she almost enjoyed feeling like a victim, and when he came, violently, with a loud, agonizing moan, she wanted to caress and comfort him, but something in his wild, hard face kept her from it.

He stood up and got dressed, still without saying anything, and she grabbed for her jeans and blouse, and just to say something, it slipped out of her: "You didn't use a condom," and he asked, "Aren't you on the pill?"

"Yes," she said, "but there are other risks, like HIV and AIDS, for instance."

He waved dismissively, "I don't have AIDS, I'm healthy."

But maybe not for long if you keep this up, she thought, but she didn't dare say it out loud, for one thing she didn't know if she could say it in English with the correct, slightly nonchalant intonation, besides, she didn't want him to think she wanted to change the subject or accuse him of something.

He had brought her back to the bus stop and explained to her how to get back to her hotel, that was all, they didn't talk about it, they didn't see each other again. That was it, nothing else.

During her last two and a half days in Israel, Johanna had tried not to think about this incident, or about the fact that he had done it without protection. Only when she got back home did she go to a gynecologist and ask her—after making sure she was bound to confidentiality, even in the case of a minor—for an HIV test. Over the next couple of days until the results came back, she almost wished she had gotten infected as a punishment, as an apology, as something that would make him the perpetrator and her the victim.

The result was negative, and her sudden relief proved to her that all the other nonsense running through her head was just mind games she was playing on herself, completely irrational, and therefore stupid and meaningless. She was glad her life had not taken a dramatic turn.

Only much later when she was able to reflect on what had

happened did she understand that both of them had been playing a game, not a fun child's game but a deadly game meant to hurt the other person's heart and mind, a game with roles reversed, as though the game could have undone something. This realization made her shudder, and she wondered if he had realized it, too, after the fact, because his desire wasn't actually a physical desire, either, but something completely different—despite the orgasm he expressed with a violent, low groan, an agonizing sound—completely different from Daniel's heavy breathing, completely different from Daniel's laughter after he comes, as though each time he's surprised by the novelty that there is such a thing.

Johanna stands up and pushes a CD into the player because she can't stand the silence anymore. *I've got to tell Daniel,* she thinks. *I can't keep it to myself any longer, no matter what happens, I've got to tell him.* And suddenly she feels so relieved, as though she had already told him, as though she already had everything behind her, she starts to laugh, the way Daniel laughs when he's had sex. *I'll tell him*, she thinks. *He'll understand, he always understands everything.*

The music lulls her to sleep, but when she wakes up from her nap in this room that has since grown dark, in this room where it's completely quiet, ominously quiet, she remembers she was dreaming about running away from something, she's forgotten what, she can remember only that she was running, just running and running.

Johanna's taken a shower, washed and dried her hair, she's put on her prettiest sweater, the blue one with the two stripes in light gray and olive, paired with black pants and the new boots she bought just a couple of days ago.

I'll make myself up like I would for a first date with a boy, she thinks, amused as she stands in front of the mirror scrutinizing herself. She's satisfied, this stone blue looks good on her, it goes with her blond hair and pale skin and makes her brown eyes look even darker, all in all she doesn't look that bad, if only she hadn't inherited this mouth with the thick lips from her grandmother. She smiles, but that hardly makes her lips any smaller. *There's nothing I can do about it,* she thinks. *And Daniel really likes my mouth,* and fleetingly she considers showing him a picture of her grandmother at some point so he knows what this kind of mouth looks like on an old woman. She pulls on her jacket and gets going, thankful that Mom is letting her take her car because Mrs. Fachinger lives about ten kilometers away, in one of the villages outside of town, out in the countryside.

That morning, after class, when Mrs. Fachinger was already packing her books into her leather bag worn smooth with time, Johanna went up to her and asked if she could talk with her. And when Mrs. Fachinger looked at her watch and muttered, "Well, unfortunately, I've got an appointment after school right now, so I have to head straight home," Johanna quickly added, "It doesn't have to be right now, whenever you have time, it doesn't have to do with school, it's something personal."

Mrs. Fachinger's face didn't show any of the surprise that Johanna had actually expected, she nodded as though it were completely normal for a student to want to talk to her in private, and she asked, "Would you like to come over to my house for tea later?" And when Johanna nodded in surprise, she said, "Today at four o'clock," and she wrote the address down.

It's a pretty little single-family house with a yard, standing between two other little houses whose lots are all as big—or small—as the others. It's obvious that the houses all used to look the same once upon a time right after they were built, but in the meantime their uniformity has been dashed by glassed-in porches, patios, carports, and different kinds of fences. Mrs. Fachinger's house doesn't have a glassed-in porch, it's painted light yellow, window boxes are hanging in front of the first-floor windows with the sad remains of withered geraniums, there is a birdhouse on a wooden post, in front of the house, her house looks broad and inviting. The fence consists of simple, white-painted slats, and the color is peeling off in spots.

While Johanna parks the car at the curb and heads over to the low front gate bearing a warning about a biting dog, she realizes that she has no idea if her teacher is married or has any children. She's amazed that she doesn't know, *we see each other almost every day but don't know anything about each other, as though there were no life outside of school and outside of these roles that the school prescribes for us.*

She presses the copper doorbell on the left jamb of the gate, over the nameplate, she can hear its piercing tone from all the way out here. Inside the house a dog starts barking, the front door to the house opens, and Mrs. Fachinger appears. She stays on the covered porch at the top of the steps holding an excited, barking dog by the collar, a medium-sized male with a shiny black coat. The lock at the gate buzzes, and Johanna pushes it open.

"Come on in, Johanna," Mrs. Fachinger says, smiling. "No need to be afraid, Bruno doesn't bite, just the opposite—he just loves guests, you'll see in no time."

When Johanna closes the gate behind her, Mrs. Fachinger lets the dog loose, and he rushes excitedly at her, jumping all around her while she follows the gravel path up to the steps. She laughs, pets the dog, charmed by his happiness. It wasn't until Mrs. Fachinger holds out her hand and says, "Welcome!" that it occurs to her that she forgot to bring flowers, but she doesn't apologize because she's afraid an apology would sound silly and stuffy.

She takes off her jacket, hangs it on a hook in the entry hall, and Mrs. Fachinger leads her into a warmly furnished living room where the table at the window has already been set, white dishes with blue flowers, a bulbous teapot on a warmer, a sugar bowl and a creamer, and a flat dish with cookies.

Johanna sits down, the dog named Bruno stands next to her and rests his head on her knee. "I always wanted a dog, but my parents thought a dog isn't a good fit for a family with a store, besides my mother is allergic to dog and cat hair," Johanna says, and immediately she thinks, *Why am I telling her that, I'm babbling like a little child.*

But Mrs. Fachinger nods sympathetically, "That's too bad," she says, "I've always had a dog." Then she picks up a cup with a spill-proof lid that Johanna hadn't noticed before, pours tea and cream into it, and says, "Excuse me for just a second, I just want to take some tea out to my mother quickly."

She disappears with the cup and a small plate with cookies into the adjoining room, Johanna hears her saying something, but she can't understand the words. She pets Bruno, and when he licks her hand with his wet tongue, she quickly wipes her fingers off on her pants, thinking, *What am I doing here, what a lame idea, coming to visit my teacher.* And suddenly she hears Mom's voice saying, "You shouldn't air your dirty laundry in public," and Dad saying, "It's not appropriate to talk about your family in front of strangers," and Grandpa saying, "Traitors to the family, they're all traitors to the family," and she wonders when he said that, but she can't recall, just that he said it, the sound of his voice still rings in her ears.

Then Mrs. Fachinger comes back in, she pours the tea, offers Johanna cream and sugar, she's a friendly, attentive host, and she gives the dog one of the cookies.

They're sitting across from each other. Johanna doesn't know how she should start, the words come out of her only with effort: "It's about my grandfather, about the store. I've got the feeling that everyone knows something that I don't know, and my father ..." She falters, takes a cookie and a sip of tea, which is so hot that she burns her tongue, and she shrugs.

Mrs. Fachinger just watches her, waiting, and then Johanna says, "My grandfather claims he bought the store honestly, and Mrs. Levin says he stole it, I just don't know what's right, the one or the other." Relieved, she takes another sip of tea, this time more carefully.

Mrs. Fachinger leans back. "I've done a little research," she says. "I suspected that you might come to me—or rather, I hoped you would ever since that meeting in Jerusalem, I've been noticing how hard this has all been on you, Johanna, but I didn't want to intrude, it's not all that simple. So, what is it that you want to know?"

"My grandfather paid one hundred thousand reichsmarks for the store," Johanna says. "I know that from my father, how can Mrs. Levin say that he stole the store from her?"

"Well," Mrs. Fachinger starts, "it often used to be the case that Jewish property owners didn't receive any of the money, you've got to imagine how things were at the time this all happened."

"Well, then who got the money if not the Jewish owners?"

"In most cases, the government," Mrs. Fachinger answers hesitantly, much more hesitantly than at school, Johanna feels herself growing impatient.

"You do know, of course, how Jewish stores were boycotted," Mrs. Fachinger continues, speaking in an obviously matter-of-fact, distanced way. "Signs were put up everywhere that said Germans! Don't Buy from Jews, members of the SS blocked people from entering Jewish stores. So, at the time, the reality was that Jewish stores were being driven into bankruptcy so that the stores could then be acquired cheaply. That was commonplace in those days."

Mrs. Fachinger pauses, Johanna pets Bruno's smooth, cozy fur, waiting for her to continue speaking. Bruno stretches and lies down in front of the radiator.

"This kind of plundering wasn't anything unusual, I think you can say it was the norm."

"So what was the story with Heimann & Compagnie?" Johanna asks. "You said you did some research?"

"Do you really want to know?" Mrs. Fachinger asks again, and Johanna says, "Yes," even though at the moment she isn't so sure anymore—what does it all have to do with her, anyway, it was so long ago—but she can't help it and asks, "Did my grandfather pay for the store or not?"

"He paid one hundred thousand reichsmarks, that's true," Mrs. Fachinger says, "with a mortgage that his wife and relatives cosigned as guarantors, too. But the Heimanns and Rosenblatts received hardly any of the money. Of that amount, twenty thousand reichsmarks officially went to the government for the Jewish property tax, which was a punitive tax ironically imposed on Jews to pay for the damage that non-Jews did during 'Kristallnacht.' Then there were two organizations called the Israelite Religious Community and the Association of Jewish World War I Veterans, and they were formally entitled to a large portion of the money as well. These organizations served as guarantors for Heimann & Compagnie, but the government froze the organizations' accounts, so no one could access the money anymore. Apparently, the Rosenblatts were able to withdraw a portion of their money before the accounts were frozen, and then they got it to the United States, I have no idea how they managed that or how much money it was, but the Heimanns didn't get anything."

"But he really did pay for the store," Johanna says, clutching at this straw that her teacher has held out, aware her protest is feeble, so weakly she adds, "If the government stole the money, it wasn't his fault."

Mrs. Fachinger leans forward to pour herself another cup of tea, her hair hangs down like a curtain in front of her face so that Johanna can't see how she's reacting to her attempts at a defense. She takes two spoonfuls of sugar and stirs, stirs for a long time, until she leans back again, brushes her hair from her forehead, and looks at Johanna almost pityingly, cautiously, without saying anything.

"I've always heard he did the Jewish owners a favor, otherwise they would have had to leave Germany without a penny," Johanna says. "My father says that, too. Maybe my grandfather and my father didn't know anything about it."

Mrs. Fachinger straightens up, and her voice now sounds resolute, the voice of a teacher who knows what she's talking about. "Your grandfather certainly knew about it, and your father must have known about it, but in any case one cannot say that he did the Jewish owners any favor, most certainly not."

"But he didn't steal the store directly," Johanna says, a final attempt. "Please, tell me what really happened."

"Unfortunately, it's not that easy," Mrs. Fachinger says. "Erhard Riemenschneider was a dues-paying member of the Nazi Party, he had held a seat on the city council as a member of the Nazi Party since 1935, that's the only reason he got the store, and what he paid was next to nothing, as they say. The owners of Heimann & Compagnie were in a desperate situation, they tried to salvage something, but it didn't work. Business was bad, that's true, but that wasn't their fault. The Nazis did everything to run Jewish stores out of business. It was people like your grandfather, Johanna, who drove Jewish businesses almost into bankruptcy, so they could walk off with them cheap. Yes, he did pay, but he profiteered from a selling price that was much too low. The one hundred thousand reichsmarks that he took out the mortgage for was, of course, much too little. Think about it, given the massive depreciation of property values during the Great Depression, no bank in the thirties would have offered a mortgage for anywhere near as much as the full value of the property, that alone should have made you suspicious."

She doesn't say anything, Johanna stares into her almost-empty teacup, the brownish rim looks disgusting.

"Would you like another cup of tea?" Mrs. Fachinger asks in a voice that is suddenly quite soft again, and Johanna nods, relieved. She can't say anything, she tries to sort out what she's heard, she can't, only one thing is buzzing in her head, *he was a profiteer, he took advantage of the situation, and Dad must have known it. "He did the Jews a favor," yeah, right, he took advantage of the predicament that he had driven them into in the first place, he got rich at their expense, a profiteer …*

A loud, unintelligible groaning comes out of the next room. "Excuse me for a moment," Mrs. Fachinger says, putting the teapot down and quickly standing up.

The groaning gets louder while the door is open, but not more intelligible, and then quieter again when the door clicks shut behind Mrs. Fachinger, then it's still.

Bruno, who has been lying on the rug in front of the radiator the whole time, trots over and rests his head in Johanna's lap, looking up at her with his wet, brown eyes. She holds a cookie out to him, thankful for the distraction, he carefully takes it with his big teeth, chews once, swallows, wags, and raises his face again expectantly. "I don't know how many cookies you're allowed to eat," Johanna says softly, giving him another, "if it were up to me you could have them all, I've lost my appetite, anyway." She pets his head, feeling the hard top of his skull under his tight skin above his eyes. "Here you go, one more," she says, and he licks her hand in thanks.

Mrs. Fachinger returns, "Sorry," she says. "My mother, she's bedridden, end-stage Alzheimer's, it's terrible. In the mornings when I'm at school, I've got a nurse who comes over, but I have to take care of her myself in the afternoons and evenings. It's hard."

"What did you do while we were in Israel?" Johanna asks.

"Oh, she was in the nursing home temporarily, it's possible to place people who need constant care in a nursing home temporarily, fortunately, because sometimes I don't know how I'd manage otherwise."

She rests her face in her hands for a moment. Johanna can see only her hair, the silvery strands that catch the light when she moves.

Without thinking Johanna says, "My grandfather was pretty confused by the end, too, he hanged himself, my father says he had a 'lucid moment' and realized what the rest of his life would be like, so …"

"I heard," Mrs. Fachinger says, lowering her arms again, her hands lying open in front of her on the table. "I think your father is right, and the decision that your grandfather made deserves respect."

"I just think it's terrible that no one talks about it in my house," Johanna says, for a moment she desperately wants to sob like a little kid, but she regains her composure.

She lifts her eyes and looks at Mrs. Fachinger. *She has a pretty face,* she thinks. *Strange that I've never noticed before, a face that's growing old in an attractive way.* And suddenly she feels as if she has to defend her grandfather to this woman who knows so much about her family. "He was a good grandfather," she says. "I loved him very much, before."

She quickly grabs a cookie to distract herself, because she's afraid she could lose her composure, she doesn't want to do that, this woman is her teacher, it's enough that she saw her that time in the bathroom at the Ticho House, that was humiliating enough. She takes a bite of the cookie, chews, swallows. The swallowing hurts, she lowers her hand, feels Bruno take the remainder of the cookie from her grip, then he goes back to his spot in front of the radiator and lies down. She looks out the window, a bird is circling the birdhouse and then flies away.

"A lot of people did that in those days, right?" she asks and hears how small and thick her voice sounds.

"Yes," Mrs. Fachinger says. "A lot of people did that. But a lot of the things that happened along those lines were not very conspicuous, not very public. Maybe a scholar got his position as a professor at a university because the Jewish professor was dismissed, how do you calculate the damages or what was gained in that case? Maybe a doctor suddenly has a waiting room full of patients every day because his Jewish colleagues aren't allowed to practice medicine anymore. There were shopkeepers who were able to enlarge their stores because the competition had been put out of business. All the way down to the little people who were able to buy whatever household items for cheap because Jews were forced to sell their property—they weren't allowed to practice their professions anymore, after all. How do you quantify all these things, there's no way. But they all took advantage of the situation, all of them, they took advantage of the injustice that people perpetrated upon other people, even most of those who were later categorized as only 'nonresisters.'"

Mrs. Fachinger hesitates, raises her shoulders, then drops them again, and she says, "There is a long tradition of this, in the Middle Ages people took part in pogroms because they owed money to Jews. It was a convenient type of excuse, kill your creditor, and you're debt-free …"

"What about your family?" Johanna asks, then wishes she had bitten her tongue. "I'm sorry, I shouldn't have asked that."

But Mrs. Fachinger smiles sadly. "You are perfectly entitled to ask that," she says. "And if it makes you feel better, it wasn't much different in our family, either. My father was also a teacher, I come from a long line of teachers, and when the Jewish principal at his school was dismissed in 1933, as were all Jewish teachers and civil servants, they offered my father a position and he quickly accepted, he was also a dues-paying party member, like your grandfather."

She raises her shoulders and drops them again, a motion that Johanna now finds very familiar, and Mrs. Fachinger says softly, "I can't even say he was a good father, the way you said your grandfather was a good grandfather. He was a tyrant, he was harsh and cruel, and until the day he died he was convinced that he had done everything right."

"Well, what did you expect your father to do?" Johanna asks. "It's not like he could have changed anything that happened, anyway, nothing can be undone, it all happened."

"Maybe he could have *talked* about it," Mrs. Fachinger says, "talked, admitted something, called an injustice, an injustice and guilt, guilt."

"You can't bring the dead back to life, no one can."

"No," Mrs. Fachinger says. "You can't bring the dead back to life, but guilt remains guilt, it isn't pardoned by pretending it doesn't exist."

She lowers her head, then she says, "That's it, pretending it didn't happen, that's what I'm mad at myself for."

"Why?" Johanna asks. "You didn't do anything, you were a child. What could you have done?"

"I could have talked about it," Mrs. Fachinger says. "If nothing else, I could have talked about it. Remaining silent made me like his accomplice, as if I had somehow sanctioned it. Talking doesn't undo anything, but there isn't anything left for us to do other than talk."

Who do you mean by "us"? Johanna thinks. *Both of us, you and me, or do you mean us Germans?* But she doesn't ask, because suddenly she recalls Mom's favorite saying: *There are truths that benefit no one.*

"I never dared to have an argument with him, to confront him," Mrs. Fachinger says, again raising and lowering her shoulders, perhaps the only sign of helplessness that's available to her. "I always found excuses for him, sometimes it was my parents' bad marriage, then the death of my brother, who died of leukemia when he was fourteen, then my father's job, his health, he suffered from ulcers, I never forced him to talk about it. And now I'm paying penance for it with my mother, who *can't* talk anymore—a just punishment, don't you think?" And softly she adds, "I've never forgiven myself. I want you to know that, Johanna ..."

Johanna is silent, looking out the window, the bird has returned, now it's sitting on the tar-paper roof of the little house, but maybe it's not even the one from before, perhaps it's a different one.

Then they hear the groaning from the side room again, Mrs. Fachinger goes over. Johanna quickly stands up, almost relieved, and Bruno gets up, trots expectantly over to her. When Mrs. Fachinger comes back into the room, Johanna has already fetched her jacket from the hallway. "Thank you so much for making time for me this afternoon," she says, offering Mrs. Fachinger her hand.

"Thank you for coming to me, Johanna. It's a sign of trust that I value a great deal," Mrs. Fachinger says. "It isn't something that I take for granted."

Johanna struggles to keep her composure, she bends over, pets Bruno, wipes her eyes discreetly, but they're dry, even though they burn and hurt.

Once outside, in the car, she starts to cry. *Why?* Actually she knows why, she's just found out what was actually clear to her, anyway, even if she didn't allow herself to realize it. She pulls over to the edge of the street at the entrance to a dirt road, and waits for her breathing to calm down again.

On the drive home she wonders why she didn't tell Mrs. Fachinger about the money she inherited, two hundred fifty thousand marks, a quarter million. *Without all the things he did,* she thinks, *he would never have been able to leave me so much money. If he hadn't been a profiteer, he wouldn't have had much more than Aunt Amalia and Uncle Erwin.*

And then she thinks, *At some point I'll get myself a dog, when I get back from Israel and have my own apartment, a Bruno,* and this idea comforts her, even though she knows that it'll be a while yet. The future isn't completely dark anymore—there is something for her to look forward to, even if it's only a dog.

Thin Ice The key grinds metallically as Johanna turns it, and mixed in with the sound is another tone, it's the high-pitched tone that her mother always adopts when she's furious, an unpleasant tone that hurts the ears. "She's your daughter," the voice yells from behind the closed door to the living room, "can't you just give in this one time?"

Johanna softly opens the front door, lets her backpack slide off her shoulder, hangs her jacket on the coat stand, and moves silently through the dim hallway.

Her father is speaking loudly, too, but he's not yelling. "That critical look she's always giving me," she hears him say, "it pisses me off, I won't stand for it anymore." And her mother responds, still ranting, "What do you expect, you scold her like a little child and at the same time you want her to have a serious discussion with you and interact like an adult ..."

Johanna had spent the afternoon with Kerstin and the others, they'd eaten a late lunch together and had a great time, but now she feels her happiness, her sense of camaraderie with her friends, melting away. And her hands, which had been waving good-bye to them just a moment ago, now hang heavily at her sides. She was just admiring the chartreuse-colored western sky at dusk with its promise of nice weather tomorrow morning, and now she's staring at the dark grain running through the living-room door like scribbly writing she can't decipher.

"Johanna," someone whispers from upstairs. "Johanna."

She turns around, forcing herself to raise her head.

Florian is sitting on the half landing up the stairs, he puts his fingers over his lips and waves at her, in the light shining from the open door to his room his hair looks so blond, almost silver. She nods, tiptoes to the stairs, pulls herself up the steps by leaning on the railing to avoid making the steps creak, and she thinks, *I'm so glad I wore my tennis shoes today.* She can hear her mother saying something, then her father again, but now, from upstairs, she can't understand them anymore, although it seems as if the voices are booming in her ears.

Florian takes her hand and pulls her after him into his room and softly closes the door. "They've been fighting for a while," he says. "I'd really like to grab something to eat, but I don't dare go down into the kitchen, I've been waiting for you to come home this whole time."

Johanna drops onto his bed, he sits close beside her, very close, and she scoots farther back to lean against the wall. She thinks she can still hear her parents' voices, but she's probably just imagining it, because when Florian asks, "Where have you been?" the voices are suddenly gone, everything is still, she can hear only Florian's breathing, the creaking of the bed and the rustling of fabric as he lies down next to her, crouching with his knees and arms pulled in. He asks one more time, "Where have you been?"

She doesn't answer, she strokes his head, lost in thought, running her fingers through his hair the way she ran her fingers through Bruno's coat a week ago.

"I was in another world," she must have said, "in a completely different world, carefree, with people my own age, it was a lovely afternoon, we had a dinner together and laughed, and

Moritz even asked me out, and we all wondered why we haven't done it more often—cooked a meal and eaten together." It was like in Israel, only a lot happier, more relaxed, they had all turned in their articles so they were free to reminisce about their trip without dreading all the writing they had to do. "You two are really incredible," Dominik had begun, "and I don't just mean like if someone runs into you out clubbing at Riverside or something, you're the coolest, nicest women in our class," and Moritz had smiled at her, nodding in agreement.

That afternoon Johanna had driven over to Kerstin's house, they had prepared the appetizers together, tahini and hummus with salad and pickles, and set the table. The main course would be cholent, a meat and bean stew that had been simmering on the stove since morning, they made it using a recipe out of a Jewish cookbook, and Kerstin had said she was thinking of maybe going to Israel, too, and working in a hospital there if she ends up being wait-listed for medical school, and Johanna had nodded and said, "Yeah, that would be really great," and thought, *She and I probably could've been good friends, too bad that I'm realizing that only now.*

Then the others had arrived, Melanie had brought two loaves of challah, and Moritz had brought two bottles of wine. After dinner they read their articles out loud to each other and looked at the photographs that they had taken together. "What a great Saturday afternoon," Moritz had said as they were getting ready to leave, then he put his arm over her shoulder and asked, "Do you want to catch a movie with me, Johanna?"

If only I had accepted his invitation, she's thinking now, on Florian's bed, *then I'd be sitting in a movie theater, maybe with a bag of popcorn, laughing while Moritz makes funny comments.*

Hanging on the wall opposite her is the glass cabinet with her grandfather's rock collection. She stares at the stones that seem so boring to her, she had never understood why he would pick one rock to keep and not the one lying next to it, and the voices in her ears grow louder, "I don't want to hear any more about it," her father says, and Mrs. Levin says, "That goddamned Nazi," and suddenly she can hear Doron's voice, too, "I'm wondering where you get the nerve to come to Israel," and Mrs. Fachinger says, "He knew it, he must have known." "Of course he knew," says Daniel, "but there are people who prefer not to hear anything, not to see anything, and not to say anything."

I should have talked to Dad right away after I came home from Mrs. Fachinger's, she thinks. She had tried to several times, but something always came up, a welcome excuse to put off the conversation, sometimes she was too tired, sometimes he was too irritable, or Mom had a headache. *Excuses, excuses.*

"Talking, expressing it, calling it injustice, telling the truth, there may not be anything else left for us to do," says Mrs. Fachinger, not in the matter-of-fact voice that she uses at school but in that other, hesitant, cautious voice, and as she raises and drops her shoulders again, Johanna scoots off the bed and says, "I'm going downstairs."

Florian leaps up and plants himself in front of the door with his arms spread out as though he could actually block her path. She laughs, but it isn't a happy laugh, it's a bitter one very close to crying. "Why don't you put on a little music, Flori?" she says. "Incidentally, I've got a chocolate bar in the drawer of my desk, you can go grab it if you want." She pushes him aside and opens the door.

She pauses on the half landing and looks down the steps, the bottom of the stairs seems so far away, as if she's the heroine of a tragedy and this is a set on a stage that she has to descend, slowly, in measured steps, so she can relay her monologue to the audience expressing her inner turmoil, using her most tragic voice and heartrending gestures—no, so she can have an argument with her antagonist—no, so she can beseech him for mercy.

She hesitates again in front of the door, remembering her script, she's been thinking about what to say for a long time, at least she knows the beginning by heart, because the script is important, as a preparation, so that they don't resort to a fight right away.

"I've got to talk to you two," she'll say, the "you two" is an excuse, a detour, it means: *No direct confrontation, please, you are both my parents, I am your daughter,* and then she'll announce that she's planning on going to Israel after graduation, a sort of voluntary service year, nothing more to it than that, you can't possibly object to something like that. She only has to find the right tone and say it just as an aside so he doesn't go ballistic right away.

All the same, she feels as if she's walking on thin ice as she opens the door and enters the dim living room where the only light is coming from the floor lamp next to the couch upholstered in green. Her mother is sitting in the armchair, her father is standing at the window. She goes to the couch, her knees wobbly, *swaying like a reed in the wind,* she thinks as she walks over the sea-grass–colored rug, but the pond that the sea grass is growing in must have frozen over because the ice is cracking alarmingly under her feet. She sits down on the couch and says, "I've got to talk to you two," just as she had prepared, in a casual tone, and then she says that she wants to go to Israel for a year after graduation.

"Israel," her father says from the window, turning around

toward her. "What do you want to do there, what in the world is going on in your head, I just don't get you. Israel, instead of starting at college and majoring in something sensible."

Sensible, she thinks. *Sensible is what you think is sensible, you have never once asked me if I'm really at all interested in the store—but that's not what this is about, let's not talk about everything all at once.* She breathes deeply once, and then she has control over herself again.

"It's a beautiful country," she says, "and I want to work in a nursing home, kind of a voluntary service year, that *is* a worthy project, you guys can't have anything against that."

"Israel," her father says slowly. "Incredible." And then he asks, "Is it because of that Mrs. Levin?"

The ice under her feet cracks louder, she squeezes her hands with her knees as though she has to hold them tight.

"Yes," she says. "I think it's because of Mrs. Levin."

"And because of him?" he asks, and the ice cracks, it breaks, and she doesn't know how deep the water is underneath her, but it isn't a mere puddle.

"Yes," she says. "I think it's also because of him." And suddenly she doesn't care about it, she doesn't care about any of it, she's just going to say it, say it to that face lurking in the shadows of the drapes. She doesn't need to see it to know that his eyebrows have drawn together and his chin has pushed out, she thinks she can even hear his jawbone pop. She presses her knees even more tightly together, so tightly that her hands hurt. "I found out what the real story was," she says out loud. "He was a profiteer, he took advantage of the situation, he enriched himself at the expense of the Jews."

It's quiet for a moment, then the voice of her father comes, imploring and ominous. "He paid for the store, one hundred thousand reichsmarks, that was a lot of money in those days."

"But the Heimanns didn't get any of it," Johanna says. "Your father knew it, and you must have known it, too. If he had really been the decent man he always pretended to be, we would not be rich, he knew what he was doing."

"Don't act so holier-than-thou," he snarls, "you're pissing me off." And she would have liked to say, *And you're pissing me off, too,* but she doesn't dare. She raises her shoulders helplessly, "That's not why I'm talking about this," she says, "but we have to admit that everything we have is based on an injustice, on a lie."

He pulls a pack of cigarettes out of his pants pocket, holds one to his mouth, the match lights up, his eyes flicker, darken, his face is in the shadow. *Since when has he been smoking again?* she thinks. *I never noticed.* It's very quiet. "And what, in your opinion, should I do about it?" he asks, more calmly now. "Should I hand everything back that we've worked so hard for, both your grandparents and us? Have you forgotten how the store has consumed our whole lives? We've worked, we've only ever worked, there has never been an eight-hour workday for us, and certainly never any five-day work week, you know that, it's always been about the store, it's devoured us. Even if everything you say is true, then we've paid for it with our lives."

He stops, the tip of his cigarette glows, flickering a warning.

She knows that he's right, or at least he's not entirely wrong, the store is devouring the lives of its owners. She's uncertain for a moment, but uncertainty is actually her goal. *Do something,* she thinks. *Do something, anything, just don't act like all this is OK.*

"What, should I give away all the money?" he asks, as though he's heard her thoughts, "or should I divide it up? How then? The good into the pot, the bad to rot? And what about you? Will you buy yourself only half a car because, in your opinion, the other half is unjust and you're not entitled to it? Do you want to live in half a room, eat half a meal? Or what percent were you thinking? And does your condemnation apply only to the second generation, but the third is somehow exempt?"

"I don't know," she says. "But it's unjust, just admit it."

"Unjust!" he yells. "Unjust! Look around you—then every possession here is unjust! Well, what is just about it if someone lands a big contract just because he has a relative or a friend in a high place, or if someone gets hired through relationships or bribery, if a guy inherits a house from an uncle who he never took care of his whole life long, is any of that just? Why do we need contracts and courts in the first place if it's so easy to separate the just from the unjust? The bill of sale for the store was rock solid, even the judge agreed, the only thing in dispute was the price. And the store wasn't worth anything anymore, anyway."

He's clinging to his old arguments, Johanna thinks, furiously. *Why doesn't he listen?* She pulls her hands out from between her knees, her fingers are stiff, the skin around the white patches where she was squeezing them has turned red, she feels the familiar urge to stand up and run away, but she has to force him to talk. "He and his whole party were the ones who drove the Jews into bankruptcy in the first place, and then they would buy the Jews' property," she says. "It was the same story for Heimann & Compagnie."

He gets louder, the cinder at the end of his cigarette glows its warning again. "You are so arrogant," he says, "arrogant and smug—and you can thank him for that, too. Only a child who has grown up in such wealth can be so disrespectful and arrogant, so merciless and judgmental."

That's true, she thinks. *Why am I accusing him? On some level I knew what the truth was, too. The moment Mrs. Levin said it, I knew it was true, I must have heard it somewhere, but I didn't want to admit it. I was always so proud of the store, I never wanted to be someone who doesn't have anything.*

"I don't want to hear about it," he says. "It's long past, at some point there must be an end to it. Talk talk talk, always talk, the whispering behind our backs, I don't want to hear anything more about it, do you understand? Maybe he made a mistake, but he who lives in a glass house …"

The silence in the room grows so stifling she can't breathe, her mother's breathing is also audible, it almost sounds like groaning. She feels as if the couch is swaying beneath her, she can't stay seated anymore. Her knees shake as she stands up, her mother grabs for her hand, her mother wants to hold her back, but Johanna walks, her knees still wobbly, past the painting of the moor landscape that's now hanging in their living room, up to the window, and stands right in front of him. "Dad, he didn't park in a tow-away zone or steal a can of caviar from the grocery store," she says. "He enriched himself at the expense of the Jews—what would you call that? And what would someone call what you did?"

"Stop it," he says, threateningly.

But she won't stop, she has thought the words too often to swallow them all now. "You lied to me," she says. "You lied to me my whole life, he wasn't doing them any favor when he took over the store, he exploited his membership in the Nazi Party to walk away with the store. You must have known. You lied to me, you lied to all of us."

He raises his hand.

"Receipt of stolen goods. That's what it's called," she says loudly, "when someone accepts something stolen, it's a felony."

She watches his hand swing down and slap her in the face. "Shut your mouth, I never want to hear you say that again."

Her mother jumps up, runs to Johanna, who lifts her hand in disbelief to touch her cheek, as though it belonged to someone else. *It doesn't hurt*, she thinks, surprised. *He hit me and I can't feel anything, I only heard the strike.* She almost laughs as her mother puts her arm around her and says something she can't understand, and then the sting is there, delayed, she lowers her eyes, she looks at his broad hand that is still moving back and forth, the powerful fingers are bent, stiff. She breaks out of her numbness, pushes her mother's arm aside, and makes her way across the room to the door. She can't feel any of the brittle, crackling ice anymore, it's melted, she's wading through a lake, fighting her way forward, breathing with relief as she closes the door behind her.

"Johanna," her mother calls after her, "Johanna," but she doesn't care. *Daniel*, she thinks. *He must be home, he wanted to study for physics this weekend, how lucky that he's taking his exam on Monday.* She grabs her jacket, it slips out of her hand, falling onto the floor. When she bends to pick it up, everything around her is spinning, she staggers but manages to put the jacket on and leave the house.

The cold fall air assails her, she's having a hard time moving forward but doesn't know if it's because of her legs or because of the sudden weakness that has seized her or if a storm has blown up. She could look at the trees in the front yard to find out, but she doesn't bother, lowering her face, she walks close along the fence.

Mrs. Levin, she thinks. *I did it, you aren't a rambling old woman anymore, I've called the injustice "injustice." But I'm not proud, I'm only sad, do you understand that? Do you know why I'm so sad?*

Daniel's mother opens the door for her. "Johanna," she says surprised. "What a state you're in! What's happened?" She pulls her into the warm hallway and calls up the stairs, "Daniel, Johanna is here, come downstairs quickly. Johanna, would you like something to drink? Shall I make you some tea?"

Johanna nods, hoping that that is a sufficient hello, she can't get any words out. Through the open living-room door she can see Daniel's father sitting in his recliner and looking over, curious. She hears a woman scream and wonders if she's screaming herself, but then she realizes the screaming is coming from the TV.

"Hi, Johanna," Daniel calls from upstairs. "I wasn't expecting you, is something wrong?"

She turns toward him and when he sees her face, he rushes down the stairs, puts his arm around her and leads her up to his room. Silently he pulls her jacket and shoes off, and Johanna lets herself fall onto his bed, thankful that he's not asking any questions. Before she closes her eyes, she can see that he really was studying, his lamp is casting a circle of light onto his desk, onto his books, his notepad.

"I had a fight with my dad," she says into the darkness before her eyes, "I told him everything, everything, and then he hit me."

Daniel lies down next to her, holds her in his arms the way her mother was holding her earlier. "I want to sleep over here with you," she says, "please?" And he asks, "What will your parents say?" She opens her eyes, looks up at him, brushes the hair out of his eyes, and smiles. "I don't care, they can say what they want."

Daniel's mother knocks on the door, comes in with a tea tray in her hand. "I put in a splash of rum," she says. "You looked like you could use some, Johanna."

Daniel takes the tray from her and sets it onto the nightstand, pushes her back out the door, and closes it behind her.

"And what will your parents say if I spend the night here?" Johanna asks. Daniel grins and says, "I don't care, they can say what they want. Come on, let's go to bed, you look like you really need some sleep." He switches on the lamp on the nightstand before he turns off the ceiling light and the lamp on his desk.

Then they lie next to each other in bed, Johanna carefully sipping her hot tea with rum, Daniel caressing her stomach and her legs. She sets the cup back onto the tray and turns out the light. In the protection of the darkness, she tells him about Doron, as much as she has the energy to tell. "I wasn't in love with him," she says. "It was something else, it had nothing to do with you, please, Daniel, you've got to believe me."

He pulls his hand away, she can sense that he's frozen, lying next to her, frozen like a mannequin. He doesn't say anything, but he doesn't throw her out, he doesn't lash out at her, he doesn't swear at her, and she thinks, *This isn't over yet, there'll be more to this, but not today, please, not everything all at once, I'm so tired.* Sleep comes over her like a comforting friend, taking her into its arms, and slipping away she can feel that Daniel is still lying frozen next to her.

Both of the kitchen windows have been freshly cleaned, Mrs. Maurer has taken advantage of the nice fall weather over the past few days, the sun is shining on the sideboard, illuminating the green cutting board as though it weren't made of plastic but of some kind of precious jewel. The smell of chicken soup is filling the kitchen, the soft bubbling sounds like a reassuring whisper, it matches the soft music on the radio, and Johanna thinks, *Of course there's chicken soup today, she always boils up some chicken soup when someone's sick, but I'm not sick.*

"Chicken soup doesn't cure everything," Johanna says.

Her mother sets an onion, a leek, and two carrots onto the cutting board. "He's sorry," she says. "He didn't mean it, his hand slipped, he said, before he drove off this morning."

"He said it to you," Johanna says, "to you, not to me."

"You can't expect everything from him," her mother says. "It was already hard enough for him that you didn't come home last night."

Johanna takes the onion, cuts off the tip, and pulls the rustling brown shell down with her fingers, something that she had liked to do even when she was little, and, as she keeps pulling, she examines the irregular stripes with their jagged edges that emerge from under her hands, until the onion is firm and white, lying in front of her. Only then does she take a knife and cut it into slices while her mother empties the dishwasher.

She's trying to get us to make up, obviously, she always does that, her striving for harmony. Mom's efforts at making everybody happy are something you can count on, abilities that Johanna has often admired her for because she makes it easier for everyone to live together—except that when Johanna's angry, these abilities are more of a weakness. Her mother thinks of everything, she doesn't leave anything to chance, she doesn't forget anything, every employee gets something on his or her birthday, not just the salespeople "who need to be kept happy," as she says, "because happy employees sell more," but even the cleaning staff, who don't directly contribute to the bottom line. They're not big gifts. For anniversaries with the company, just a bouquet of flowers, a box of candy, a bottle of cognac, not exactly original but still ... *She sends Uncle Hubert little packages for his birthday and Christmas,* she thinks. *Don't be unfair, Johanna.*

The stinging smell rising up from the sliced onions makes her eyes tear up, they're pouring down her cheek. She wipes her sleeve over her face, she's OK with crying for no reason. "Why do you always defend him?" Johanna asks, as if addressing the dishwasher her mother is hunched over. "Why don't you ever take my side, or do you also think I should shut my mouth and not wake any sleeping dogs?"

"If it were only that easy," her mother says behind her, shutting a cabinet door, perhaps a bit too hard. "Of course I understand what you're saying, but I understand what he's saying, too, he's never had anything else—a child without a mother—and now you want to take his pride in the store away from him, too? What will be left for him then?"

"Why did she kill herself?" Johanna asks, abruptly.

She hears her mother fill up a glass of water and drink it, then she turns the radio off. "No one knows," she says. "She was forty-five, sometimes women have hormonal imbalances, women of that age often suffer from depression."

Her voice sounds hesitant, questioning, as though she's waiting for an invitation to keep talking, as though there were something more.

"Do you really believe it was just because of hormones?" Johanna asks, still with her back to her mother. "Uncle Hubert said he was having a relationship with a saleswoman back then, do you think that was it?"

She turns around. Mom has sat down at the table with her elbows on the edge, resting her face in her hands, in front of her the empty water glass, next to it a folded newspaper that a fly is sitting on, motionless like in a still photograph, as though someone had stopped a movie. Mom's fingers are clean and white, with carefully painted nails, on her right hand the wide, golden wedding ring is sparkling, on her left hand the diamond ring that Dad had given her for their twentieth wedding anniversary and that she's worn ever since.

The fly moves, crawls over the edge of the newspaper onto the tablecloth, and a soft drumming interrupts the stillness, Florian has put in a CD, much too loud if you can hear it all the way down in the kitchen.

Johanna goes across the kitchen to grab the mincing knife out of the drawer. Her mother doesn't look up. *At least she's not pretending like she knows everything the way she usually does,* Johanna thinks, caressing her mother's hair as she walks by, a fleeting touch, but her mother lifts her head, makes a crooked, embarrassed smile.

"Your father never knew about the mistress at all," she says, "at least he never mentioned it. He thinks it was something else."

"What, then?" Johanna asks. She rocks the mincing knife back and forth in even movements over the onion slices, listening tensely behind her.

"The trial," her mother says. "The heirs took Grandpa to court in 1960, that was the year she killed herself. Your father isn't ready to talk about it, I think, he secretly held Grandpa responsible for the whole thing, but of course he couldn't admit that."

"Why not?" Johanna asks. "His mother kills herself, how can he just accept something like that, he must have thought about why she did it, how could he have carried on with life otherwise? He was seven years old when it happened, kids can already understand a lot at seven. And why didn't he talk about it later on with Grandpa, when he was ten or twelve or fifteen, why has he always remained the dutiful son, kept his mouth shut, even now? Don't you think maybe it was just easier for him? It's not like he had to worry about whether he would inherit anything."

Johanna hacks away at the onions, tears pouring out of her burning eyes.

"Johanna," her mother says sharply. "Don't assume so much. He was a kid, and he didn't have anyone else besides his father, he had to get along with him. Every child needs someone to love him, and that's why a child is ready to accept, and excuse, a great deal." She pauses for a moment and adds, somewhat more softly, "And to forget."

Johanna turns around. "I didn't mean it like that," she says, and then she asks, "What was he like, actually, when you first got to know him, was he this pigheaded even then?"

Her mother smiles, "No, I don't think so, I didn't notice it, anyway, but sometimes I'm not sure if I judged everything correctly back then. He was so lonely and tragic."

"And so rich," Johanna says, tipping the minced onion from the board onto a dish, she takes the leek and peels off the outer leaves.

"True," her mother says. "At the time the store still belonged to his father, and it wasn't as big as it is today, but he was the only son, in my eyes he was rich. And I was just a young salesgirl, at the end of my training period, it was flattering to me that the boss's son was interested in me, and the flattery worked, too. You can't understand, you don't know how it is to wake up in a family where everything is scarce, not just money, but happiness, too." She hesitates, then she adds, "And love. My parents were small people who had also been devoured by their work, by work and worry, there wasn't much energy left for dreams."

"And was he your dream?"

"He has a lot of advantages that you forget in your anger. He's thoughtful and loyal and generous, and he had the same yearning for a beautiful home and family that I had. That connected us, the yearning for a proper place to call home, we wanted to make everything better."

Johanna raises her face and looks out the window over at the spruces, her father had built a tree house spanning them, a long time ago, after Florian was born. "Your own empire," he had said when it was done, "so that there's a place for you to get away to sometimes when your little brother is filling the house with screams, a tree house just for you, and no one's allowed to go up if you don't explicitly give them permission."

The light pine wood has darkened over the years, the ladder and boards have come to match the trees, but she remembers how often she really did withdraw there, up into her own empire, alone or with her girlfriends, especially Nicole. They would sit up there for hours, reading and talking, and sometimes even doing their homework.

"And he paid a high price for his wealth," her mother continues, "a child with no mother, a child with a father who has nothing but money in his head. You got to know him only as an old man, but believe me when I say Grandpa used to be different, he was coldhearted and stingy, an insufferable cheapskate."

"Stingy," Johanna says, amazed. "But I never noticed anything like that."

"Only because you never needed anything from him," her mother says, "and because you're not particularly demanding, either. But I can well remember what a short line he kept us on when the store still belonged to him. Especially in the early years, I often used to look like a panhandler. But that's how he was, a cheapskate, and maybe he wouldn't have gotten as far as he did otherwise, he turned every penny over twice before he spent it, especially if I was the one who wanted something."

"I never knew that," Johanna says, and her mother says, "There's a lot you don't know. But that's how it is sometimes, children see only what they want to see."

She stands up, takes the pot with the boiled chicken off the stove, the soft bubbling suddenly stops. "You two *have* to make up," she says. "Somehow or other we have to move on, this just won't do."

Johanna sets down the knife, wraps her arms around her mother, presses her close to her, lays her head on her shoulder. Her mother's hair is soft like fleece, her smell mixes with the smell of the chicken soup, her mother runs her fingers through Johanna's hair, *her left hand,* Johanna thinks, *the one with the diamond.* "Oh, Mom," she says. "Things'll be OK again, I don't know how yet, but I won't run away, you don't need to worry about that, I want to go to Israel just for one year, nothing more. But I can't promise you that we won't ever fight again, I'm not a kid anymore, and I won't let him treat me like one, either."

Her mother keeps stroking her hair, a tender, familiar movement. "You'll find a way," she says. "You're much stronger than me, I'm not worried about you, I'm worried about us, about our family, do you understand? You and Florian, you are our life, you two are actually what we have achieved, not the store."

I wouldn't say that's been clear from your actions, though, Johanna thinks, but she doesn't say it out loud. She steps back and over to the sink, washes the onion smell off her hands. Out of a sudden inspiration she says, "Give me the key to Grandpa's house, I want to drive over there again. Can I take your car?"

"But the furniture is all gone," her mother objects. "The house is empty, the agent is showing it to potential buyers, there isn't anything left to see."

"I just want to go into the garden," Johanna says. "It's important. The key ... please?"

"It's hanging on the key rack," her mother says, "and the car keys are on the bureau."

Johanna gives her a kiss, grabs her coat, takes the key, and leaves the house.

On the drive she thinks about how often she had gone over to his house, usually on the bus, and how she had always looked forward to seeing him, to his questions about school, his pride in her good grades, back when he was still just her grandfather and she didn't know anything about the goddamned Nazi. *Black and white*, she thinks. *I've got to try to see the shades of gray, too. He wasn't only the beloved grandfather, but he wasn't only the goddamned Nazi, either.*

And then she thinks, *I would have liked it better if he had stolen a can of caviar from the grocery store, I would have liked it better if I hadn't inherited any money from him,* but then she corrects this thought immediately, *if I had inherited less money from him, clean money,* and then she can hear Daniel saying, "*Clean money,* what is that supposed to mean?" "When you earn it with the labor of your own hands," she answers. "The money that Mrs. Tschernowski got is clean." Daniel laughs and says, "Bleeding-heart crap."

She pushes the thoughts of Daniel aside, that'll have to wait, he's hurt, of course he is, but she can explain it to him, in the end he'll understand. And then her grandfather is there again. She loved him, as a child, as a teenager, she always loved him more than her father, who often seems so strange to her, so absent, that she can hardly imagine him without the intermediation of her mother. *Grandpa*, she thinks, and the word hurts, like a splinter you press deeper and deeper into your foot with every step you take on the spot where it keeps hurting, under the skin. *Grandpa, if only just once you had said, "Yes, I'm sorry," just once, then I could have kept on loving you. But your silence was a justification, it repeated the injustice every day, you let it happen again every day, everything could have been completely different if only you had admitted it.*

The gate still creaks when she pushes it open, the tall grass is lying in brown tufts on the ground, pressed down by the falling leaves of the nut tree, a squirrel is climbing up the trunk, then leaps into the bushes along the fence and disappears. An earthworm is winding its way out of a hole in front of the toe of her shoe, its gray intestines show through its pink skin. And suddenly she remembers one Sunday, it must have been a Sunday because they were all out in the garden together, her parents and her grandfather. She was picking daisies when Florian, who was just two or three at the time, was suddenly standing in front of her, his hands behind his back, and he said, "Open your mouth and close your eyes and you will get a big surprise!" She closed her eyes and opened her mouth, expecting a piece of candy or chocolate. But it was an earthworm. She spit it out, disgusted, and Florian laughed at her shriek, but not for long because she jumped up and pounced on him until their grandfather broke it up. He took her onto his lap and explained to her how beneficial earthworms are, and she cried and said, "but not in my mouth!"

Johanna shivers, it's a beautiful, sunny fall day, she's freezing from the inside out. She zips up her jacket, folds the collar up, and looks over at the front door. The house is withdrawn, cold, the shutters are all rolled shut.

She takes a big step over the earthworm and walks to the bench under the apple tree. On its bare branches there are still a couple of fruits hanging, like little Chinese lanterns, but most of them have fallen off and are rotting in the grass and on the gravel, but the sun is clearly still warm enough—there are wasps flying around the fruit, crawling over the brown spots where the mold is breaking through like white blossoms. The weeds have grown tall, there are still a couple of scattered dahlias in bloom in the beds, the others are withered, their browned heads drooping down.

She can see him in front of her, how he was kneeling the last time between the beds, she watches him raise his face and look at her. "That's how the world works," he says. "The children and grandchildren always have to take care of their fathers and grandfathers. As though their fathers and grandfathers were something better than they are."

"That's not the point," she contradicts him, wiping a couple of dried leaves off the table with her hand. "I only want to understand why you did it."

"Understand," he says. "Understand. You can't possibly understand, you don't know what you're talking about, you have no idea how things were in those days, time ..."

"That's not enough, time isn't an explanation. It's about the store."

"It was my only chance, I would have never gotten another one. The Heimanns would have lost the store either way. If I hadn't done it, someone else would have." He wipes his brow with his hand, leaving a stripe of dirt, his eyes becoming bluer. He rips off a couple of withered flowers, holds them up out to her and says, "I only did it for you, so that you would be better off."

She looks at him. She would love to believe him, but his face is displaced by the image of an old, bitter woman who dreams of her violin, saying, "He stole everything from us." Johanna's eyes move over his stubbly chin, over his neck, which had grown so thin in his last few months, as thin as Mrs. Levin's neck.

At this moment she understands that it wasn't any sense of justice that drove her to touch up the image of Mrs. Levin in her head, it wasn't about any favor that she owed this woman, a kind of atonement—Johanna was just doing herself a favor, she wanted to appease her own uneasiness, her own guilty conscience, or that of her grandfather. *Historical revisionism*, she thinks, *that's what I'm doing,* and she can't stand the thought. She lowers her eyes before this face, this woman's face, which is suddenly so naked and old and vulnerable before her, she no longer needs to see the reproach in it, not now.

Her grandfather is still holding out the flowers to her, a gesture of atonement that she cannot accept. She turns her head, looks over the fence at the wilted meadow that runs up to the woods, to the silken blue sky with a couple of clouds sailing across it, and she hears him say, "We were young in those days, we believed in the great ideals, the songs, the campfire, the camaraderie. Everyone went along with it, but believe me when I say we didn't know about the bad things. They took advantage of our naïve enthusiasm, we were misled. If we had known then what we know today …"

"I've heard and read that so many times before," she says. "No one knew anything, no one was personally responsible, secretly everyone was against it, but no one could do anything about it, it was a different time then."

"Some sympathy … ," he says, "just a little sympathy," and she asks, "Do you think you earned any sympathy?"

When she turns her face back to the flower beds, he's disappeared. *He's dead*, she thinks. *Dead, dead, dead. Death is the measure of all things,* she read that somewhere. It sounds like a very old and very wise saying, although she doesn't understand it. And then she thinks, *I don't want to understand it, either, even if it is wise, I don't want to.*

After a long while she stands up, stretches, picks an apple off the tree, and sticks it into her coat pocket, and only later when she's back sitting in the car does she notice its strong, sweet scent.

The weather report was talking about a cold spell, possible snowfall down to the lower elevations of the foothills. It's not snowing now, but you can tell that the snow is coming, too early for this time of year. The sky is gray and opaque like an old, faded wool blanket, hanging so thick over the trees that you almost feel as if you need only stand on your tiptoes to touch it.

They're walking next to each other, the winding footpath up the mountain to the grand old hunting chalet. Daniel suggested it, and she said yes immediately, she would have said yes to anything after these past few days of not talking to each other—anything so long as he wanted to be with her—although it's a stupid idea for them to go for a hike in this weather, the sky is so overcast there won't be much to see, and who knows if the pub at the chalet will even be open.

The trees are bare, their dark branches stark against the sky, blurred like in an old drawing. Daniel's blue jacket is the only spot of color amid the gray that surrounds them, everything is gray, the ground, the fallen leaves, the bushes, the grass, varying shades of gray. Daniel is setting the pace, he's walking quickly, actually rushing forward, upward, she's having a hard time keeping up with him. His shoulders are raised, his hands buried deep in his pockets, and he's not speaking, as though they were strangers who happened to be going for a hike on this autumnal path in the woods together at the same time.

Normally they would have been holding hands, as soon as they were alone, but now her hands feel so superfluous, she pulls them into her sleeves, like a muff. They hurt with their longing, and it's so cold she's having a hard time breathing. It's quiet, an oppressive quiet punctuated only by their steps and breathing.

The last time they had walked along this path was in the spring, just before her trip to Israel. *It hasn't been all that long, really, a good half a year,* she thinks, *but it seems like half a life.* Back then the world had looked different, light green, cheerful, and she remembers how they had made love behind a bush, she imagines feeling the warm grass under her back again, the smell of damp moss filling her nose, and her sense of loss becomes unbearable, filling her and taking away her breath, she can't keep on.

"Don't walk so fast," she says to the blue back in front of her. "Wait up."

Daniel stops, turns to face her. His cheeks are red, his eyes are looking right through her, his lips quiver as though he wants to say something, but it's only his breath flapping them. *How handsome he is,* she thinks, and for a moment she forgets the loss, walks up to him, and hugs him. He holds still. They stand there for a while, she feels his breath in her hair, on her ear, warm, familiar. "I'm so sorry," she says, and he says, "What are we supposed to do now, what do you want," and she says, "You."

She raises her face and looks at him. Daniel stops staring off into the distance, and their eyes meet, and she says, "Too bad it's so cold ..." As he takes her hand, he starts to smile, the smile that she loves so much. "It's never too cold," he says, pulling her along behind him into the trees, and when they're far enough from the path, they stand hugging each other as though it were the first time. Through his thick clothes she can feel his warmth, his body that she knows so well. "It's never too cold," he says again, pushing her back against a tree. And when she sees his uncertain expression, she laughs and turns around. She wraps her arms around the trunk and holds still while he opens her jeans with his fingers, stiff and clumsy from the cold, he pulls them down, and enters her from behind. Her fingers grope over the trunk, which is smooth and damp and getting warmer and warmer until her fingertips start to glow. She hears moaning and doesn't know if it's her or Daniel. She comes and he comes and they both laugh, and suddenly everything is the way it's supposed to be, everything's all right despite the gray and the cold. As they straighten their clothes, he says, "Next spring we'll do it in the moss again."

Hand in hand they keep walking, emerging from the woods, they see the city way down below them as they walk the last few meters up to the pub at the chalet, it's open, the warmth hits them, envelopes them. A cat rubs past Johanna's leg, purring, she bends down, and her fingers, still bearing the memory of the smooth, damp tree trunk, run over its soft fur. Then they sit down in the warm, elegant lounge, at the window, with a view over the city, their hands wrapped around the warm teacups.

"You're lucky we're open today," the manager says. "We're catering a company's anniversary party later this afternoon, otherwise we wouldn't be here at all, in weather like this."

They look at each other. The warmth flows from the teacups into their fingers, their arms, their whole bodies, and now they can say what they wanted to say the whole time, for all those days he was avoiding her. "I'm sorry I hurt you," she says. "I didn't want to hurt you, the thing with Doron just happened."

"Nothing just happens," she hears, without him speaking, but she knows that's what he's thinking, she's heard him say it many times before. *Why isn't he saying anything?* "I wasn't in love with him," she adds, uncertain, and then he interrupts her, saying, "I think we shouldn't talk about it anymore. It's past, and if you say it didn't have anything to do with me, then I believe you."

"It didn't have anything to do with you," she says, and thinks, *But I went with him, and if it had gone differently it might have had something to do with you,* and she imagines Doron in front her, standing in that dorm room at the camping stove, preparing Arabic coffee with *hel.* At that point it was still undecided, it could have gone differently.

Daniel takes her hands into his, his fingers are long and narrow, delicate like a girl's.

"I'm scared we'll end up breaking up if you go to Israel," he says.

"It doesn't have to be that way," she says. "If we don't want it to, and it's still seven months off, more than half a year."

"Will you get together with him when you're in Israel?" he asks.

She shrugs. "I'll visit Mrs. Levin, that's for certain, and maybe I'll run into him then, but I won't start up anything with him, you can be sure of that." She imagines Doron in front of her again, his face is smug as she climbed onto the bus, and she turns toward him again and thinks, *I really don't want that, even if I liked him at first, but after what happened, it won't work anymore.*

She looks out the window, the city is shrouded in mist, you can hardly see the church steeples, to say nothing of the medieval roofs in the center of town, the store and the houses to the right on the east slope are nothing but light gray spots in the dark gray of their yards.

Daniel, who has turned to see what she's looking at, says,

"The city looks different than usual, strange, as though we had been gone a long time and were just back for a visit."

Johanna nods. The cat jumps onto the bench next to her, climbs onto her lap, grinds its claws into her pants, she can feel the sharp little points through the fabric, she lifts the cat up, holds it in her arm like a baby, and rubs its belly.

"Next year we'll both be gone," he says. "You'll be in Israel, and I'll be at some university or other. Strange, isn't it, we've always lived here, you and me, and now the end is in sight."

She laughs, imitating her old Latin teacher, "*Non scholae sed vitae discimus,* have you forgotten that? I wish it were time already, I'm ready to go."

The softness of the cat's belly makes her hands caress it all the more, she smiles.

"And what about us?" asks Daniel. "Then we won't see each other anymore."

She puts the cat back down onto the bench, no substitute for Daniel, there is no substitute for him, only now is it clear to her what it will mean for her not to see him every day, he won't be standing at the steps anymore, his hand resting on the round stone cap, his one knee pushed forward, waiting for her. She imagines herself in Israel, standing on the Mount of Olives, *the most beautiful view of the Holy City,* and feels herself yearning for him. She looks at him as though he had become a stranger to her, as though she hadn't seen him for a long time. "You could come visit me in Israel," she says.

"Yes," he says. "I'd like that. To tell the truth, the past few months I've regretted not joining the school history project and working on the annual, I had thought the ecology project would be more exciting, but it wasn't."

"Mrs. Fachinger brought the galley proofs into class today

and passed them around," she says, "so we could read everything through carefully one more time, we could still change something if need be. And she said we should spend some time thinking about what we've gotten out of the project."

"And?" Daniel asks. "What did you get out of it?"

The cat has rolled up next to her leg, purring, Johanna can't hear it, but she feels the vibrations in her hand resting on the cat's back, a soft, rhythmic rumbling. "Trouble," she says. "That was my first thought, that it just caused me a lot of trouble, and that I shouldn't have joined that group. But then I realized I was wrong, even though I experienced things I would've preferred not to go through. 'There are truths that benefit no one,' as my mother says."

"That's a load of crap," Daniel says. "There are truths that people don't want to know, that's for sure. But your mom's saying could also be an excuse for not saying something out loud." Now he looks the way he always does to her, a little smug, a little mocking.

"Sleeping dogs," she says.

He nods, "Sleeping dogs."

"I've been thinking about something," she says. "I think we should pay Mrs. Levin the purchase price again, the one hundred thousand reichsmarks, this time in deutsche marks. I think we should pay it together, my father, Florian, and me, because we're the ones who inherited the money from my grandfather."

Daniel lets out a surprised whistle, the manager comes over and asks, "Would you like anything else?" And Johanna says, "Another tea, please," because it makes her uncomfortable that the woman interrupted her preparations behind the counter to come see what they needed. The woman disappears again. Daniel looks at her, without saying anything, and she quickly continues, "Mrs. Levin doesn't have much money, I think. You can tell from her furniture." *You can also tell from her teeth,* she doesn't say it, it would have seemed disparaging.

"You pay and the case is closed?" Daniel asks.

"No," she says. "That's not how it is, it can never be like that, the injustice has happened, and it will always be an injustice. It is just an attempt to make things easier for Mrs. Levin. Do you have a better idea?"

"No," he says, "I don't. But somehow it bothers me that you can do it just because you have enough money, as though that settles it. Money isn't any atonement."

"But that's why doing nothing and keeping the money isn't a solution, either."

They're silent, looking out the window again, the manager brings over a cup of tea and sets it on the table in front of Johanna.

"There just isn't any right solution," Daniel says while Johanna takes the teabag out and sets it on the saucer. "And your father is prepared to pay the money?"

Johanna shrugs. "I haven't talked to him yet, we're still kind of staying out of each other's way right now. But I'm not afraid of him anymore, strange, isn't it, I think it's harder for him right now than it is for me, I almost pity him, as though he were a child who doesn't know how to get out of some stupid situation he's created for himself. Like with Florian when he was up to some kind of mischief."

"Actually, you'd have to split the money between Meta Levin and that Mr. Rosenblatt from New York," Daniel says.

"True," Johanna says. "But the Rosenblatts have enough, I think."

"Do you want some type of justice or to just do something nice for Meta Levin?"

"I don't know," Johanna says. "I really don't know. It could also just be that I want to do something nice for myself."

"My parents were well-off," Mrs. Levin says. "More than that, they were rich. Until Hitler came along I wanted for nothing. We owned the largest clothing store in town, Heimann & Compagnie, on Marktplatz, an ideal location, today it's called Riemenschneider's ..." The money might make your life easier, Mrs. Levin. It won't bring anything back, it won't undo anything that's been done, but maybe it can be a small atonement.

"Will she even accept the money?" Daniel asks. "Maybe she'll think it's charity, maybe she's too proud."

Johanna raises her shoulders and lowers them again. "No idea how she'll react," she says. "I think about her so often, but in reality I don't know her at all, not what she's really like, I think I've just kind of made her up, like a dream."

She looks out the window, vainly searching for the roof of the store on Marktplatz in the gray of the city. "I can't even remember her face that well," she says. "Just her hands and her voice. When I think about her, she looks like Mrs. Neuberger."

They're silent for a while again, there isn't anything else to say, not now at least. The first streetlights flicker on down in the city, dusk comes early on days like this. Daniel pulls his wallet out of his bag. "Come on," he says. "We've got to get going so we're back down the mountain before it gets dark."

Hand in hand they walk through the woods down into the city. The cold has eased. On the edge of the path, a pale stone catches a bit of light under a fern. Johanna picks it up, it's round like a bird's egg, she wipes the dirt off it, and puts it into her pocket.